CAD IN

CLOTHING
AND TEXTILES

A Collection of

Expert Views

Fashion Design and Product Development
Harold Carr and John Pomeroy
(0632 028939)

Introduction to Clothing Manufacture
Gerry Cooklin
(0632 026618)

Knitted Clothing Technology
Terry Brackenbury
(0632 028076)

Materials Management in Clothing Production
D J Tyler
(0632 028963)

Metric Pattern Cutting for Children's Wear
Second Edition
Winifred Aldrich
(0632 030577)

Metric Pattern Cutting for Menswear
Including Computer-aided Design
Second Edition
Winifred Aldrich
(0632 026359)

Pattern Grading for Children's Clothes
The Technology of Sizing
Gerry Cooklin
(0632 02612X)

Pattern Grading for Women's Clothes
The Technology of Sizing
Gerry Cooklin
(0632 022957)

The Technology of Clothing Manufacture
Harold Carr and Barbara Latham
(0632 021934)

CAD IN CLOTHING AND TEXTILES

A Collection of
Expert Views

EDITOR

Winifred Aldrich

OXFORD

BSP PROFESSIONAL BOOKS

LONDON EDINBURGH BOSTON

MELBOURNE PARIS BERLIN VIENNA

Copyright © Winifred Aldrich 1992

BSP Professional Books
A division of Blackwell Scientific
  Publications Ltd
Editorial offices:
Osney Mead, Oxford OX2 0EL
25 John Street, London WCIN 2BL
23 Ainslie Place, Edinburgh EH3 6AJ
3 Cambridge Center, Cambridge,
  Massachusetts 02142, USA
54 University Street, Carlton,
  Victoria 3053, Australia

Other Editorial Offices:
Librairie Arnette SA
2, rue Casimir-Delavigne
75006 Paris
France

Blackwell Wissenschaft-Verlag
Meinekestrasse 4
D-1000 Berlin 15
Germany

Blackwell MZV
Feldgasse 13
A-1238 Wien
Austria

First published 1992

Set by Best-set Typesetter Ltd in
  Hong Kong
Printed and bound in Great Britain
  by Hartnolls Limited, Bodmin,
  Cornwall

DISTRIBUTORS

Marston Book Services Ltd
PO Box 87
Oxford OX2 0DT
(*Orders*: Tel: 0865 791155
     Fax: 0865 791927
     Telex: 837515)

USA
Blackwell Scientific Publications, Inc.
3 Cambridge Center
Cambridge, MA 02142
(*Orders*: Tel: (800) 759-6102)

Canada
Oxford University Press
70 Wynford Drive
Don Mills
Ontario M3C 1J9
(*Orders*: Tel: (416) 441-2941)

Australia
Blackwell Scientific Publications
(Australia) Pty Ltd
54 University Street
Carlton, Victoria 3053
(*Orders*: Tel: (03) 347-0300)

British Library
Cataloguing in Publication Data
CAD in clothing and textiles.
  1. Textile products. Design. Use of
     computers
  I. Aldrich, Winifred
  677.022

ISBN 0-632-02977-3

Contents

Contributors

CAROLINE ASHBY, 128 Shakespeare Road, London W3 6SW

DOUGLAS COOPER, 48 Duchy Road, Harrogate, Yorks HG1 2EY

ROZ DAVIES, Courtaulds Textiles, 100 St Pancras Way, London NW1 9NY

JANE DEVANE, 76 Conduit Street, Gloucester GL1 4TU

STEPHEN GRAY, 18 Cowper Road, Harpenden, Herts, AL5 5NG

KAREN MACHIN, Royal College of Art, Kensington Gore, London SW7 2EU

PETR ŠÍPEK, c/o J Carroll, TCS Ltd, Enterprise House, Lloyd Street North, Manchester M15 4EN

JOHN HARVEY VALLENDER, 278 Brook Lane, Kings Heath, Birmingham B13 0TQ

GAVIN WADDELL, Rathlin, Pittville Circus, Cheltenham, Glos GL52 2PX

TONY WALSH, Complan Technology Ltd, 7 Milestone Court, Town Street, Stanningley, Leeds LS28 6HE

CLIVE WALTER, Marks & Spencer plc, Michael House, 47–67 Baker Street, London W1A 1DN

PHIL WIGHT, Little Haw Lane, Shepshed, Leics LE12 9LN

Introduction

WINIFRED ALDRICH

Winifred Aldrich is a practising designer, experienced in both industry and education, and now working in computer aided design at the Nottingham Fashion Centre. She was previously a lecturer in Loughborough and London in clothing design and pattern cutting and has published three books on the subject. She has recently completed her Ph.D in CAD in clothing design at Nottingham Polytechnic, where she is continuing her research in this field.

Two events took place in September 1990 that concerned me. First, I asked a group of seventy first year textile students beginning HND and Degree courses, 'How many of you have used a computer?' Less than 25% replied, 'Yes'. Of this small group only one student had used computer graphics. Secondly, at the Fabrex Exhibition of 'Textile Designers 1990', I asked to be shown some examples of student textile work in which computers had been used; it seemed that only one piece of work could be found to show me. I spoke to many students displaying their work at the show, a surprising number of whom thought that computers were only useful for technical work and stated that they had not been given an opportunity to experiment with computer aided design (CAD) in design projects.

It seems clear that many students are still entering colleges as computer illiterates; they should not be leaving colleges in the same condition. I believe that the use and discussion of the value of CAD in clothing and textile design is an inseparable part of any current course which is preparing students for a career in either industry or the craft market. It is apparently not the case in many colleges. Perhaps this book will help to lift the barrier of ignorance that appears to surround many textile and fashion departments. This barrier may exist because available knowledge of CAD in clothing and textiles is sparse. It often has to be sought among alien, highly technical computer literature that is only marginally useful. Clothing or textile journals are more fertile sources, and some technical books on clothing manufacture offer practical descriptions of processes; but rarely can you find literature that tells you what it is like to work with the technology or that offers well-argued yet sometimes conflicting attitudes towards it.

Talking about computer aided design is as difficult as talking about the process of design. Discussions of complex concepts, particularly those attempting to describe activities in the visual arts, face communication problems that can only be solved by metaphorical expression. This excites a few and leaves the majority ignorant of the 'idea'. Thus many ideas have a circulatory limit. It is often more useful when searching for the meaning of a word or expression to look at the field in which it is being used. To the participants in that field, use and communication of the word or expression is its 'true' or required meaning at that time. A concept has only a 'true' meaning in the context it is being used; instead of concern about definition, gaining an understanding of the ideas and activities in which CAD is enmeshed would seem to be more fruitful.

My work with student designers given free choice of use of the technology, together with my own personal work, has convinced me that people who say 'CAD is only a tool' have only observed it, or used it in a very limited way, or have rejected it aesthetically or mentally. Such rejections must be respected, but they should not be seen as generalisations. In my research work I found that a student's visual intelligence appeared crucial in their interaction with CAD in the design process, both in competence and means of expression. There were startling contrasts between students who produced immediate realisations of ideas, students who worked structurally, and students who endlessly refined work. When given a choice each student's understanding and use of CAD was different.

I appear, in my work, to exploit the chameleon characteristics of CAD, its amorphous qualities and capacity to be changed and moulded into many different *directed* forms. This is part of its appeal. I am also attracted by the intrinsic quality of the media – glass and light – and I am intrigued by the opportunities to transform a graphic idea on the screen into different forms of output, and by integration with other media. I appear to squander time exploring elements of software with no immediate application; but it is this time that is probably the most valuable. The possibilities are mentally recorded or merged into the software; they may be the *connections* for the design problem that has not yet been conceived. The best solutions often occur when I am engaged on an undemanding but related task – in fact, what appears to be 'messing about'. They come when thoughts are directed away from the problem but still held in some unconscious form. A deadline is often not the problem it would appear to be; in fact, it seems to provide the engine of discovery. Work that is protracted often appears to be inferior.

Observations of the practice of design within the tensions of a commercial environment have shown that CAD need not be a restriction or an unacceptable complication. However, in one's own work there has to be a high degree of personal control over the 'seductive revision' and 'insistent pace' of the technology. But the technology only *offers* alternatives and speed. The selection of work, and a rhythm of work that allows the mind to wander, is a skill; it is knowing 'how' and a resistance to the continual visual prompts. The use of CAD has, in fact, given me more time to work with ideas; it has widened my visual and practical experience; it has given me access to a new medium and to some textile practices that I would have been denied if I had been working manually. I believe that at present CAD has become an integrated part of my process of design. But this is just my personal experience; there are other experiences and other contexts.

A group of people, very knowledgeable, highly respected and working in many fields of CAD, have collaborated in this book to give their perspective of CAD and describe their use of it. Their work covers a wide spectrum: companies who write computer software for clothing and textiles; companies who sell or advise on CAD systems; a CAD bureau; companies who have invested in CAD; designers and technicians using CAD; college lecturers teaching with the technology; and finally some independent views from people who have had varied experiences and interests in the field. The book's contributors should not be seen as some kind of fundamentalist CAD movement seeking conversions; they are simply attempting to dispel some of the mystique or fear that can intimidate or limit a designer's experience of a new phenomenon. It is a phenomenon that, undoubtedly, will have a major effect on design careers in the future. I would also like to thank Kathleen Farrell for the technical index.

THE
SOFTWARE
DEVELOPER

Chapter 1
Writing and Developing Software for CAD Clothing and Textile Systems

STEPHEN GRAY

Stephen Gray, a mathematics graduate, started his career with British Telecom where he gained experience of computer aided design as an executive engineer making printed circuit boards. After eight years with BT (during which time he took a year out to gain a masters degree in Computer Science) he moved to an American company, Aydin Controls, where he specialised in producing software for computer graphics applications in the military and power supply industries.

In 1984 he was one of the founder members of Concept II Research, a software company offering low cost systems to the general CAD market. His specialism in the clothing and textiles market grew from a meeting with Winifred Aldrich. Working together with vastly different backgrounds and without funding they demonstrated the potential of cross-disciplinary teamwork by producing ORMUS FASHION.

Introduction

Writing good software for any application is difficult – writing for the clothing and textile industry is exceptionally so. Pattern cutters and computer programmers are not natural bedfellows; the former tend to have an artistic background and the latter a scientific one. But collaboration between them can produce really effective software that is powerful in its application and is fun to use. The main challenge of writing for the industry is to appreciate and capitalise on the different perspectives of the computer software writer (programmer) and the user (pattern cutter).

Software is what makes a computer system work. It is sometimes known as a program. In practice software usually means a collection of programs each performing a specific task. Software has to be geared to the industry in which it will be used. To write good software the programmer has to understand the industry, its methods and of course the computer system itself. It is not surprising that the majority of computer applications are in the fields of science and engineering, because many computer experts have backgrounds in the broad scientific subjects and therefore are well placed to provide useful programs to their own community. It is still surprisingly rare to find a programmer with a background of fashion or textile design.

A computer is only as good as its software, and then only as good as the user. Therefore to write software for the clothing industry the author needs to get inside the mind of the pattern cutter or textile designer and understand what tasks they find difficult, boring or time-consuming and identify how a computer.system could assist them. A computer system is characterised by the functions that it can perform (e.g. grading or marker making); these are limited by the hardware (e.g. can it cut out cardboard) and are controlled by the software. In writing software for the industry the author therefore has to bear in mind three primary features:

- the functions that the user will require;
- the functions that the hardware can be made to perform;
- the ability of the person who will operate the system.

This final point is extremely important and there are certain broad assumptions that have to be made about the user's knowledge of their craft and his or her ability to use a computer. The computer is no miracle worker and is only a tool in the user's hands. The effectiveness of the tool depends both on its original design and on the way in which it is used.

The remainder of this chapter will concentrate on the pattern cutting side of the business. The comments are equally applicable to textile design applications which can often be simpler to write and comprehend.

A specification

The first task of any software writer is to decide what to do and how to do it. This is a combination of analysis and experience: what tasks does the author wish to perform with the computer system and what practical limitations exist?

The specification of requirements must be written down clearly and comprehensively and must be understandable by both programmer and user. Every possible effort will be made to limit the specification to really useful functions with no frills. Getting these foundations laid down permits future enhancements without altering the original goals. Too often a good idea is ruined because the author lost sight of the original requirements. A good specification provides the basis for the documentation that needs to accompany the system and also for internal notes, test specifications and other support material.

In the clothing and textile industry the majority of software has been written for marker making. The reasons for this are twofold. Firstly the task is well defined: the aim is to lay down pattern pieces on cloth, minimising the amount of waste material. Secondly, the input and output methods are quickly identified: the user traces in (or digitises) existing pattern shapes which are manipulated on the system and are then output either to a pen plotter to produce a paper marker or directly to a cutting machine.

In writing software for more demanding aspects of the industry (e.g. a pattern design system) the task is more complex and the creation of a specification becomes more difficult and is more essential. It is important that the specification is created by collaboration between the user and the programmer. One of the fundamental reasons is the different perspective of the computer software writer (or programmer) and the user (pattern cutter). Writing software for this industry is difficult, partly because of the task in hand and partly due to the communication barriers between these two individuals.

The problem is best explained by example, so consider a standard bodice block (Fig. 1.1). There are two very different ways of looking at this and the two have to be married together to produce successful software for the industry.

The pattern cutter's perspective

The block itself gives information about the patterns that it can generate: it has a size (length, width, etc.), a dart, a round neckline and two notches. These features are used by the pattern cutter to make modifications according to personal taste and design objectives. They also show how the piece will be joined to others when the garment is assembled. In addition to the single block pattern there are associated ones (a back, a sleeve, etc.) and changes to one piece frequently dictate the ways in which others can be adjusted.

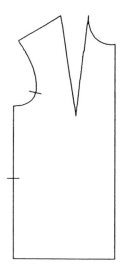

Fig. 1.1. A bodice block with a dart.

The computer programmer's view

The block is seen as a series of lines and curves each of which has a measurement. Looking more deeply these can be reduced to a set of co-ordinates that are used to generate the pattern.

The most notable difference between the two perspectives is the meaning associated with the lines on the page. A programmer needs to have the purpose of each explained and then needs to comprehend how each can be used. Consider a standard pattern cutting exercise of 'swinging the dart'; this term makes instant sense to the designer but has to be explained to the computer programmer who would view the operation as a geometric function of moving lines about a fixed point (a standard two-dimensional transformation problem). The operation is shown in Figure 1.2.

This example is one simple exercise in pattern cutting. There are many more in pattern manipulation alone, without considering the requirements of grading and marker making. Going outside the 'normal' pattern operations (for example writing software to perform gathering) vastly extends the required understanding of the programmer.

Another important point in writing the specification is consideration of the diversity of the markets into which the software will be sold. The clothing and textile industry is broad, and good, flexible software will have appeal across a wide range of markets. It is worth developing ideas of the ways that the software needs to be written. There are three main sections: the data (or information that needs to

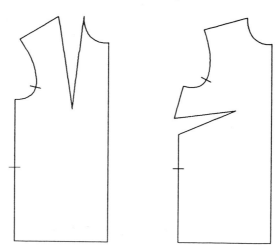

Fig. 1.2. Swinging the dart.

be stored); the user functions (the operations that can be applied to this information); and the user interface (or way in which the functions are accessed).

The database

Data means the information that needs to be stored on the computer system. In simple terms it means the collection of points, lines and curves that generate the pattern.

Using the same bodice block as in the last section (Fig. 1.1), the computer needs to have a unique way of storing and recalling that shape. The most straightforward way is undoubtedly the best: each pattern piece needs to be stored by a name that both the user and the computer can understand; within that name are stored the points, lines, curves, etc. that comprise the shape. For example the block might be stored in the following format:

Pattern piece name: bodice

Draw a straight line from 5, 5 to 30.5, 5 (the hem)
Draw a straight line from 30.5, 5 to 30.5 59.85 (the centre front)
Draw a straight line from 5, 5 to 5, 44.1 (the side seam)
Draw a curve from 5, 44.1 through 10.51, 47.54 to 6.25 60.6 (the sleeve)
Draw a straight line from 6.25, 60.6 to 16.8, 67 (the shoulder)
Draw a straight line from 16.8, 67 to 20.65, 41.6 and another from 20.65 41.6 to 23.8, 67 (the dart)
Draw a curve from 23.8, 67 to 30.5, 50.85 (the neckline)
Draw a straight line from 3.5, 25.6 to 6.5, 25.6 (the side notch)
Draw a straight line from 9.05, 47.85 to 11.98, 47.23 (the sleeve notch)
End of data

All other pieces can be represented in the same manner, basically a list of instructions or 'recipe' that is used to create the piece to specific dimensions. A whole set of pieces can then be saved together in a file.

This is analagous to manual methods. A file contains individually named pieces (e.g. back, side, etc.) and these pieces are each made up of lines, curves, etc. that join specific co-ordinates together to form the shape. The equivalent manual method is one hanger for a garment containing cardboard templates of pattern pieces each of which is named (e.g. back, side, etc.) and each of which has a specific size.

A computer system is, of necessity, well structured and well organised. It can impose a discipline on a user (e.g. insisting that all pattern pieces are named with precisely six numeric characters) or it can work in harmony with existing manual methods. Poorly written software will impose the discipline and frustrate the user; good software is sympathetic to existing practices. Generally, if the user is well organised before installing a computer system they will have little problem adapting their ways to those of the particular system chosen.

This imposes a strict regime on the software writer though: knowing the ways in which information needs to be retrieved is essential when writing a specification. For example, a pattern cutter thinks of pattern pieces by name (e.g. sleeve) with an overall shape and size, not as a series of lines, curves, notches, etc. linking points together. The programmer needs to organise a method whereby a sleeve can be recalled instantly and where different types of sleeve can be stored without confusion.

A mathematical consideration has to be borne in mind throughout the design of the software: the accuracy of the information that needs to be saved. This has a great effect on the way in which information will be stored and on the speed at which it can be accessed. There is no point in maintaining artificial levels of accuracy, and the pattern cutter will probably be confused if he or she is given measurements to 5 decimal places of accuracy when they normally work to the nearest half a millimetre.

Input, functionality and output

There are three main components to this section: data entry (how information is fed into the system), data manipulation (the operations that are performed on the information) and data output (how the information is extracted from the system).

Input

The input methods are associated with the user interface and indicate the ways in which information (data) will be fed into the machine. It is very important that these are sympathetic to the ways that are well understood by the user and it is the responsibility of the author to understand these methods and provide a computerised version. In the fashion and textile industry it is therefore essential that the programmer understands the artistic basis of many methods used on a day-to-day basis. The input methods must also be compatible with the hardware available, for example the size of a digitiser will limit the size of pattern piece that can be traced into the system.

The specification will identify which method is appropriate and the task of the software writer is to determine how the hardware (e.g. digitising tablet or scanner) will be controlled and how the input information will be read and stored. This is crucial as it affects the way in which data is represented inside the system, which in turn limits how that information can be manipulated and output. The design of the internal data format is usually in the hands of the computer programmer and is rarely fully understood by the user. However, the more the programmer understands about the ways in which the system could be used, the more comprehensive the data base and the more flexible the operations that can be performed on it.

Functionality

The ways in which information is manipulated are really the key to effectiveness of the system: the more powerful the operation the more time that can be saved over and above manual methods. As an example, consider the operations of putting a pleat into a skirt (Fig. 1.3). The first point is the observation of the manual methods (a real challenge for the computer programmer) and then the derivation of the key information that is input to the process.

Following on from this is the analysis of the manipulation that occurs (cutting the pattern, moving it out by the pleat distance and then drawing in the new lines that make up the ends of the pleat). Then comes the difficult bit: writing the software to perform the iden-

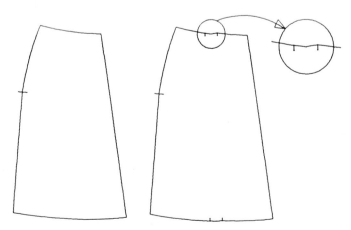

Fig. 1.3. A pleat construction.

tical operations with a simple-to-use interface. Implied in this simple description are many important decisions that are not apparent on the surface, for example the direction in which the pleat will be folded, as shown in the ways in which the pleat ends are displayed.

The information that the software will require is:

- position of pleat line;
- pleat distance;
- pleat direction.

It is the task of the software writer to provide these functions in an easy-to-use form.

Output

The computer system is absolutely useless without the ability to obtain something out of it. There are two main methods: hard copy (a print on paper, acetate or similar of the information stored in the system) or direct output to a machine that controls a process such as cutting cloth.

The simplest output is to a pen plotter which draws lines on card or paper. Plotters come in all shapes and sizes: some can take rolls of paper, others only take cut sheets. Some require specialist media and others can take standard pattern cutting cards and papers. The software must be written to control the output device, providing the user with results according to their requirements within the capabilities of the machine.

The whole output process can have its own limitations, for example a machine that cuts with a knife blade needs time to sharpen the edge every so often and the computer programmer may need to build into his software a check to ensure that this happens after the appropriate time. Since each machine has its own characteristics there is often the need to drive several output devices from one piece of software, and this is normally determined by the provision of separate 'device drives' for each type of output machine.

The user interface

Having specified the general requirements of the system there are a number of specific issues that have to be considered. First and foremost is that of the user interface. This term is often misunderstood, but what it really means is how will the user of the system tell the computer what to do next.

Computer systems have many different types of user interface, methods such as pull down menus, pop-up menus, icons, windows, etc. It is the task of the programmer to discuss these with the user and identify the one most suited to the application. There is no golden rule that covers the user interface, other than common sense. The usefulness of individual functions is determined by the ways in which the user interface is presented and these functions should be sympathetic to existing manual practices.

In the example in the last section the functions for making a pleat were outlined; the user interface determines the way in which the user will select the function and input the required information. This will take the form of a selection process: the user must choose to make a pleat and will then respond to various prompts that allow the specific information – pleat distance, direction of fold and precise position – to be input to the system.

Putting it all together

It is essential that the software writer understands the requirements of the market into which the product will be sold. To write effectively he or she needs cross-disciplinary skills: maths, computer science, art, pattern cutting and a bit of engineering too! Since it is rare to find all these skills in one individual it becomes obvious that the only practical way to work is in a small group. In fact good software development implies good teamwork. It is essential that both the 'look' and 'feel' of the software as well as the functionality are right, and this is really only possible when writer and user combine together in a working partnership. But although the emphasis is on teamwork, it is important to realise that there is a supplier/customer relationship: the pattern cutter is the customer while the computer programmer is the supplier.

This perspective may seem one-sided and the question may be asked: 'Why doesn't the pattern cutter need to understand how the computer system works in the same detail?'. There is a strong argument against this. The user needs to understand only the principles of working the system, e.g. data organisation, how to use specific functions, limitations that are imposed by the type of machine, programming considerations or similar; the detail can be regarded as a 'black box'.

Programming decisions such as the choice of computer language or data format are often just confusing. Knowing the reasons why a function is important helps the writer to provide the user with a really effective, easy-to-understand tool. An elementary exercise like measuring along a curve has far reaching and very important implications for the pattern cutter: it is an easy function to write but needs to be presented carefully so that it is easy to use. Adding a seam allowance is a simple function to describe but is very difficult to write since the mathematical formulae depend wholly on the way in which information is stored and used. There are many specific cases that have to be investigated before a general rule emerges. Grading is another function that requires careful study before it can be written correctly.

The conclusion is simple: it is not easy to get it right first time. To create software that is useful, supportable, expandable and hardware-independent requires a mixture of very special talents.

Having written the software there needs to be an intensive period of test, trial and feedback. This too is an essential part of creating a software product and is one that is easy to overlook and push to the background. Once a program has been written it needs to be tested against its original specification: does it do all that was written down and are there any points that were not covered in the original document? After this first level of testing (which is normally performed by the software writer) it needs to be put on trial with a limited number of users who will perform real work and record all the problems that they encounter. This process is known as 'Beta' testing. Their feedback is used to hone the software into a really useful package available to the whole industry. The broader the audience the greater the feedback. The closer the supplier is to the customer the greater the influence of the feedback on future product development and enhancement.

Other considerations

The computer expert also needs to advise the user about the hardware on which it is all to run. This has a major influence on the overall cost of a system to a customer, as well as having a direct relationship to the speed of operations, the amount of information that can be stored and the future expandability of the system.

It should be expected, or even demanded, that the format of data (i.e. the precise detail of the database) is available to all users. Although this information is probably not needed by the user it is a guarantee of independence. The customer needs to ensure that the information he or she creates and stores can be transferred to other systems should the need arise. This facilitates communication between companies and also guarantees that the customer is not tied to one vendor for CAD requirements. Hardware independence is another major consideration; the customer needs to have the right tool for the job and should be specific about the size, speed and quality of the input and output they require. These factors will determine the specific types of hardware.

One of the questions that the software writer must consider, therefore, is that of objectives: is the system to be of general application or is it to be specific to the industry and to the hardware chosen? Nowadays there is absolutely no reason why a system should be tied to specific hardware. There are so many aids to the software writer that the hard work of re-writing for another machine is a simple matter of re-compilation.

There are two obvious choices for the central element of any CAD system (i.e. the computer): the IBM PC compatible machine or the Apple Macintosh. Both have their good and bad points. Although the Macintosh is excellent for desk top publishing it lacks many of the features that make it relevant to the gamut of activities in the clothing and textile industry. Consequently the majority of software in this industry is written for the IBM PC environment. Other options include specialist hardware which is both expensive and inflexible. No computer programmer will choose to limit the hardware on which his or her package will run without very good reason, so software is increasingly becoming available on the standard PC hardware. To help understand the hardware requirements it is worth identifying the elements that make up a system. There are two basic types of CAD system: one for pattern cutting and one for textile design. These are shown in block diagram format in Figures 1.4 and 1.5.

Usually these two functions are divorced from each other: a system can either perform pattern manipulation or it can be used for textile design. To perform both functions separate systems must be purchased because few companies have integrated their pattern cutting and textile design packages. Good software will allow one set of hardware to run both programs.

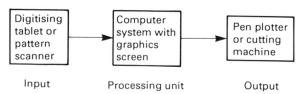

Fig. 1.4. Pattern cutting configuration.

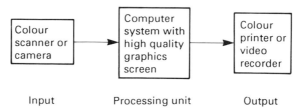

Fig. 1.5. Textile design configuration.

The author must resist the temptation to provide functions that are a by-product of the technology without thinking about their practical use to the industry. Many poorly written packages are difficult to use and demand an unacceptable knowledge of computer jargon on the part of the user. The application of high technology need not demand the use of high calibre, computer literate users. The software writer must bear in mind the ways in which new users will be trained on the system and must always consider their requirements when writing for the industry. The user will find that the computer system needs to be treated as a new medium, similar to but distinct from existing manual methods.

Practical experience

I can only be subjective here and use my own experience in writing the first version of the ORMUS FASHION package. Looking back I can appreciate just how naive I was when I first collaborated on the project with a designer/pattern cutter. I knew nothing about patterns or textiles and had to learn fast. I now think that I know a lot about pattern cutting and after taking art classes at night school have an appreciation of design, but I have never had time to put it all into practice. I understand the ways in which garments are assembled and I am slowly gaining the pattern cutter's eye – namely the ability to look at a shape and criticise it constructively: 'That collar line is wrong and the centre front needs lowering', or even: 'That sleeve will never fit into that bodice; it needs more fullness'. But progress is slow and is really only gained by practical experience. It is what the trainee or apprenticeship schemes used to provide, and something that no vendor can sell: namely experience.

One point that continues to occur though is how much I do not know! As my experience increases I comprehend more and more about the business and identify more and more areas where specialist knowledge exists. To write software for the industry one needs to have a wide range of skills and it is therefore essential to have contacts in all the right places. I have been lucky and have worked extensively with colleges. I have been able to acquire a lot of knowledge by day-to-day contact with students and staff at all levels. Unfortunately, however, there is never time to learn formally the practical and artistic skills necessary to design garments and textiles.

As a supplier of a computer system it is possible to see areas where many companies duplicate work unnecessarily. The division between design and production means that patterns are frequently passed out of the studio and are never seen again by the original designer. The process of grading is frequently done by someone who did not know how the pattern was originally constructed, and therefore mistakes can be made and not picked up until the garment is assembled. An outside eye can provide a wonderfully objective view of where a company can benefit in its working practice, simply by understanding the procedures involved in taking a design right through to production. There are many examples where spin-offs can be made once a CAD system is installed. Consider the process of bra grading: the principles of this process are difficult but once understood they can be used to generate such items as wire charts or lace outline details from the original pattern shapes.

A supplier should work with the customer, building a long-term working relationship to solve problems in all areas of design and production and helping to identify more and more of the areas where CAD technology can add benefits.

The future

Undoubtedly the most exciting and difficult area for the software writer is three-dimensional design. It is still exercising some of the best brains in the world. However, the complexity of specifying their work precludes its acceptance by pattern cutters. The vast number of mathematical calculations involved in making 2D to 3D and making 3D to 2D transformations, (mimicing the ways in which designers work with flat patterns and the dress stand), make it very difficult to operate in a 'user-friendly' manner. Until this barrier is overcome, the usefulness of 3D software will have limited appeal to the pattern cutter.

Conclusion

At first the task looks straightforward, but with increasing knowledge it becomes clear that the task is far more complex than originally imagined. Development takes place in a team comprising a minimum of two experts: the computer programmer who needs to understand manual methods for designing patterns, grading, lay planning and textile design, and the pattern cutter who needs to appreciate the power of the computer system, to understand the principles of data storage and manipulation and who needs to form an analytical approach to his or her work to capitalise fully on a system.

A computer cannot replace a good pattern cutter: it is simply a tool to help them do their job even better. The industry mixes skills from many different areas and CAD technology is just another of these skills. The frustration with writing any software for the industry is that one gains an overall perspective only in retrospect and better approaches to software can usually be identified with the benefit of hindsight. Creating the first version of ORMUS FASHION was highly enjoyable and the product has been successful. It has of course developed significantly since the early days and, like all good software, it continues to grow. This process never stops and good software needs to evolve as new opportunities occur and new technology permits.

Writing software for the clothing and textile industry is exciting and stimulating but very time-consuming. It demands a perpetually open mind and a desire to make art and science work together. The computer programmer can derive enormous satisfaction from writing really useful, time-saving functions and seeing them in use by a creative designer. Working together they can push forward the boundaries of technology as their mutual knowledge increases.

Chapter 2
Software by Design

Caroline Ashby studied Printed Textiles at Chelsea School of Art from 1975–78 before attaining an M.Phil in Constructed Textiles at Middlesex Polytechnic in 1985.

She became involved with CAD in 1985, and continued active involvement in its use and development, working in an advisory capacity for research and development as well as freelance designing and lecturing. This experience led to her current position as Textiles Systems Manager at Palazzo Computer Graphics Ltd, where she advises the technical team on software development for the clothing and textile industries, runs CAD training courses, and assists companies in selecting technology to best suit their needs.

Introduction

Cast your mind back to your first glimpse of 'painting with light' on a Computer Aided Design terminal. Where were you? What were you doing there? What were your first thoughts about this new phenomenon? Did it thrill you? Excite you? Interest you? Or did you think merely that it was just another electronic gadget to clutter our technological age – that it would not catch on?

Did you stop to wonder how it was possible to copy an image so quickly, to flip it, rotate it, fill it with brilliant translucent colours, all within seconds? Did you wonder how this so-called computer came to work like this? Did you ever wonder how the program was compiled, and who was delegated to create an acceptable aid to assist the design process?

To the layman, software is perhaps seen as a computer 'buzz' word and many may not know its true significance. In computer terms it describes a highly intricate mathematical process which, when packaged as a finished program, provides the user with a powerful means of control for completing a specific task quickly and effectively. The 'blood in the veins' is perhaps an apt definition.

As a designer, trained traditionally in both printed and woven textiles, I have found it of immense interest and a great opportunity to be involved in the forefront of software development for CAD systems for the clothing and textile industries. This chapter is based on personal experience and observation, supported by much detailed information from colleagues – the computer experts as well as fellow designers. It is intended to provide an insight into the technical intricacies and parameters of using CAD in these industries, not only to aid current CAD users but also to provide inspiration to others who are interested or may benefit from becoming involved.

Many traditionally trained designers still hesitate to use CAD wholeheartedly, in the way they would naturally pick up a crayon or paintbrush. Over the years they have tended to respond in a number of different ways to the idea of freely using CAD. Some cannot wait to get started, sensing immediately that here is a tool to really assist the daily design routines. Probably the majority are intrigued by the idea but their interest goes no further, often simply because an affordable design system is not available for training for any length of time. Many disbelieve that a computer can actually aid the design process at all, and indeed some completely reject the idea with such views as: 'Computers are machines in boxes and have nothing to do with design or artists' materials, and anyway I am a designer and I do not need a computer'. End of story.

This last response appears to come most from the older generation who frequently say that they are too old to learn about computers.

Naturally, within all these groups there are exceptions to the rule, and importantly there is a small, growing sector encompassing a cross section of professional activity and age, who can be seen as the clothing and textile CAD pioneers, seriously committed to the future development and implementation of CAD within these industries.

From a software engineering viewpoint, limited understanding of the traditional design processes as well as the specific market areas – be it clothing, printed or constructed textiles or embroidery – can often create a gulf in communication between computer technologist and designer and/or production technician, causing a somewhat restrictive software program to result. Limited funds for research and development can also be a cause of this, together with a simple lack of specific development policies within the large software organisations

To provide the type of specialist design software required by the users within these different market sectors, a close union must be formed between software engineer and design and production specialist, since the ultimate success of the program is dependent on effective communication in the development stages. The software and hardware companies must be well informed on the specific design and manufacturing requirements of the textile and clothing industries so that they are able to provide the customer with the most up-to-date and effective product, along with reliable support and training.

This chapter will illustrate, in designer terms, some of the major computer considerations, software or hardware, and advantages or disadvantages to the design process, of which CAD users should be aware. It is hoped that identification of what the computer can and cannot do from a technical viewpoint, will provide a basis from which the CAD user can become more familiar with the true capabilities of such a sophisticated tool, so that some of the mystery, and in some cases fear, which continues to exist, can be overcome. Once this is achieved, designers can start to push the technology to its creative limit, hitherto unseen to any degree, which in turn is likely to influence the type of design imagery seen in the 21st century.

Technical parameters

After examining some general computer technicalities, this chapter follows the design process, i.e. conceptualisation, manipulation and production. It is intended to provide the CAD user with a simple means of reference.

Figure 2.1 illustrates a personal computer (PC) design system featuring typical hardware technology: a scanner, computer, 14 in text monitor, keyboard, digitising tablet, 19 in colour monitor and colour printer, all of which enables the designer to complete the design process electronically.

Fig. 2.1. A PC-based design system.

The computer

Probably the one component more shrouded in mystery to the designer than any other is the computer itself, which can be seen as the nerve centre. Without it, all other components remain inoperative. A valuable exercise for any user is to see inside the computer box, to gain an idea of the basic workings.

Inside every graphics design system is a particular type of so-called graphics board, usually a rectangular circuit board covered in electronic bits and pieces, known as chips and processors and the like. Depending on the make of design system used, a graphics board can be slotted in and removed as simply as loading or unloading a plate from a dishwasher. Graphics boards have to be treated with respect; they are costly and form a vital, integral component on which the software is run. Today it is possible to buy not only standardised graphics boards, manufactured by the computer giants, but also custom-built graphics boards from specialist hardware manufacturers.

The other major components within the computer are:

(1) the central processor unit which effectively operates software programmes; it fetches, decodes and executes instructions through active RAM memory;
(2) the storage memory, into which information can be inserted and stored for future use on a hard disk inside the computer or on floppy disk (either 5.25 in or 3.5 in);
(3) the input and output lines to enable information to be taken in and out of the system, such as from scanners, or to printers;
(4) the power supply.

Monitors

The monitor is the display screen for seeing either data or graphics. Some design systems require only one monitor, others two, depending on the complexity of the software program and the particular graphics board being used. Monitors are made up of thousands of tiny dots, through which the graphic imagery is displayed by means of 'pixels' or 'picture elements', which on the graphics screen is the smallest element to be seen and controlled individually. Monitors vary as to the resolution – the total number of pixels which can be seen over the entire screen at once. Therefore the more pixels your monitor can handle the better the design imagery will look, providing the graphics board is compatible in terms of resolution.

Every addressable dot on the screen is numbered for convenience, and an important point is that software must be written to run on a rectangular shaped screen, which in itself is a technical parameter. Monitors are seen in the computer trade as being at a 4 to 3 aspect ratio, which can cause limitations from a mathematical viewpoint.

The colour image is made up of a combination of three basic colours: 'red-green-blue', or R,G,B as it is known. Inside every monitor are three electron guns, each of which handles the production of one colour.

There are two methods of refreshing colour screens, known as interlaced and non-interlaced. Interlaced displays first the even lines of visual data from the top to the bottom of the monitor, followed by the uneven lines. Hence only half the visual data is seen at one time and is usually displayed at a rate of 25 times per second. The visual effect is that the screen image is shimmering slightly, identical to any television picture seen today.

Non-interlaced operates by displaying each line of visual data in turn, from top to bottom, refreshing the whole screen at a rate of 50–90 times per second. The impression is that the image is completely still and unaffected by any flickering. Naturally this type of flicker-free non-interlaced graphics board and colour monitor is far more suitable for design work.

Monitors are measured diagonally across the screen to determine their working dimension, and generally vary in size from 12 in to 19 in and increase in price accordingly. The 19 in display may cost around the £3000 mark but is by far the best for creating and visualising artwork as it enables larger scale designs to be seen, and also simulates more closely a designer's traditional workspace.

Digitising tablets

The digitising tablet is the device which helps the designer create and edit the design on the monitor, and consists of a flat board which is positioned in front of the monitor and attached to the computer with a cable. Each tablet is accompanied by a pen, or a puck – a device incorporating a cross within a glass sight, with a number of function buttons. Some design systems support the use of a 'mouse' rather than a tablet but from a design viewpoint a pen is preferable to the mouse or puck, since it emulates the designer's traditional tool kit.

Most tablets vary in size from around A5 to A3, or even larger which can be useful if artwork is to be traced on to the system via the tablet. The 'active' workable area is not necessarily the whole area of the tablet, and often it takes designers a little time to gain precise control of this aspect.

Accompanying pens vary also, and it is worth testing different types since the right 'feel' aids design performance. Some pens tend to be rather insensitive and seem to need more pressure to activate them. Conversely, some are ultra sensitive. Some pens are attached to the digitising tablets via a flex, and some are cordless. There are also pressure sensitive pens which give the designer a little more creative freedom.

The keyboard

The use of the keyboard to aid the design process can be most beneficial, since many commands can be controlled by individual keyboard letters, enabling the task to be completed more quickly than using complicated sequences of pen movements. Most design systems running their own specialised software use the keyboard to activate functions within the paint program, in their own unique manner. For example, to select the whole screen area using Noble Campion's Cameo Paint software, the designer can actually place a rectangle around the whole screen area, or press A for all on the keyboard, which is quicker.

In addition, the keyboard is naturally a vital tool when creating text within the paint program as part of the design process, for example, for casualwear placement prints or for saving images quickly to hard or floppy disk, for storage. Hence the keyboard should be viewed as an aid to the design process, and not just as part of a 'typewriter'.

Resolution

Probably one of the most difficult areas to understand when starting to use CAD is resolution. This describes the number of addressable points which can be represented visually and is termed 'dots per inch', relating to the number of dots measured over an inch in the same way as the unit measurement for structuring woven textiles is warp ends and weft picks per inch or centimetre.

Every hardware component along the design process generally supports a different resolution, or dpi (dots per inch) as it is known. Colour scanners read visual images at a maximum of 300 or 400 dpi. Graphics boards support varying resolutions depending on the particular type of board. The resulting dpi seen on screen by the designer varies according to the size of the monitor.

Table 2.1. Common resolution variables.

Graphics board	Onscreen resolution	Monitor size (in)	DPI (approx.)
Standard VGA	320 × 200	15	24
Enhanced VGA	640 × 480	15	50
Super VGA	800 × 600	15	65
Video display (broadcast)	768 × 576	15	64
High resolution	1024 × 768	19	70
	1280 × 1024	19	90
	1600 × 1200	19	112
	2048 × 2048	19	166

Table 2.1 identifies some current personal computer graphics boards, their onscreen resolution, example monitor sizes, and the resulting dpi seen by the designer. The figures for onscreen resolution (640 × 480 for example) represent the total number of dots or pixels seen across and down the monitor.

In computing terms the width and depth of the screen are known as the X and Y axes respectively and represent the columns and rows of pixels which make up the whole screen. Since each pixel can be addressed separately, each has an X and Y position on the screen which acts as a guide for the software engineer as the program is written. Hence the higher the resolution, the finer the image quality will be on screen.

A further resolution variable is that every colour printer available on the market today prints out at a specific dpi. For example, some print at 160 dpi while others print at 300 dpi, using perhaps a maximum of 8 colours combined in such a way as to produce a range of hundreds or thousands of further colours. The total number of colours which can be produced from different printers varies according to the particular printing method used. An immense number of variables exist, therefore, with each hardware component, which in turn controls the manner in which the image has to be produced – a technical parameter.

It might be suggested that all hardware should be standardised to a specific dpi, but this in itself would create enormous creative restrictions and in addition would put many hardware companies out of business. Furthermore, input and output devices such as scanners and printers are not restricted to textile and clothing use alone but are employed across the spectrum of business activities.

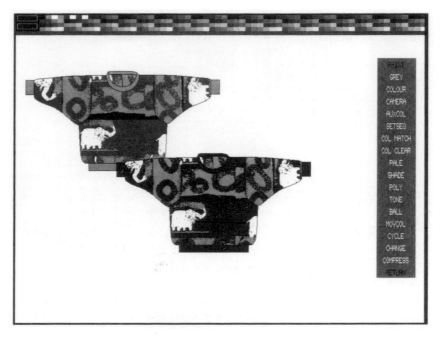

Fig. 2.2. User interface showing the colour palette and menu (The Cameo Paint Program, Noble Campion Ltd).

General software terms

In support of the hardware identified above, there are general software terms and operations which aid a designer's understanding.

User interface

From a software viewpoint the user interface describes the manner of control of a software program by the user. In general, software programs are provided with a standard operations procedure, usually displayed in the form of a series of menus or lists which allow the user to select a specific function to complete a particular task.

The visual appearance of the user interface varies considerably with different design systems, but the principles of control are the same, allowing the user to activate the various software routines. There is a current trend for many software programs to be operated by means of pop-down menus, accompanied by icons or symbols representing the function's action. For example, to fill an area of an image with colour, the icon displaying a paint pot is selected. This type of user interface is standard to all Apple Macintosh technology.

More specialist paint programs are operated by user interfaces individual to the particular software company specifications, and will
vary.

Rasters and vectors

Images can be displayed on screen in two fundamental ways: a raster
or vector display.

From a design viewpoint it is important to understand the differences, and the benefits and restrictions of each, otherwise confusion
and frustration can result because certain creative operations are
difficult or impossible using one or other type of display. All CAD
systems are referred to as raster based or vector based, and to the
layman the differences are simple.

Rasters

Raster images are displayed on screen as a series of dots or pixels.
Each pixel can be lit up independently from as few as 256 simultan-
eous colours to a maximum of a few million on screen at any one
time, enabling complex, high quality multicoloured imagery to be
achieved when displayed on higher resolution monitors.

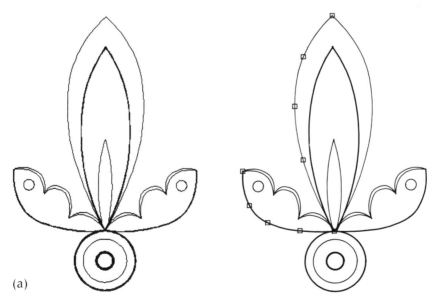

(a)

Fig. 2.3. Visual differences of a line image drawn on (a) a raster based
system, (b) a vector based system.

Vectors

Vector images comprise lit vectors or 'line segments', which when joined together form fine quality smooth lines, often displayed in one colour only. Outline shapes can be created very simply, each made up of a number of control points which can be manipulated easily and effectively to alter the image.

Essentially therefore, every shape created becomes an independent component part made up of a number of control points, as Figure 2.3 shows. Subsequently the component parts can be filled with solid colour.

Table 2.2. Major benefits and restrictions of raster and vector displays.

Display type	Visual representation	Benefits	Restrictions
Raster	● (pixel)	Images can be complex and highly coloured.	At lower resolutions image outlines are shown as jagged or stepped.
		Between 256 and 1.5 million colours can be seen on screen at one time.	Fine outlines can break up when scaling image.
		Extensive range of 'painting' functions possible, e.g. colour enhancing, cutting and pasting, soft airbrushing.	
		Good for scanning and cleaning up scanned images, and image capture from camera or video input.	
		Full control over each pixel on monitor.	
Vector	▬ (line segment)	Efficient at drafting, measuring, and scaling outlines. High quality printed and plotted results.	Usually only up to 256 colours available.
		Easy manipulation and layering of images.	Very limited 'painting' facilities.
			Unable to scan in and clean up scanned images, unless very simple.

Table 2.2 identifies both the major benefits and restrictions to the designer of these two display types. At a glance it is possible to see that the raster based display is technically more advanced for the input, manipulation, and subsequent output of a wide range of visual imagery, which can be simple or complex. This is because the images are made up of tiny multi-coloured dots, providing the designer with flexible 'painting' facilities and allowing a considerable amount of freedom for visual creation.

Naturally there are restrictions, the major one being that the edges of the imagery are distinctly 'jagged', like a series of stepped blocks, when seen on a lower resolution monitor or output from certain colour printers. Where fine smooth lines are an integral part of the design, achieving an acceptable visual quality without 'jaggies' can be difficult. Solving this problem means going to much higher resolutions or dpi on the monitor, so that the irregularity of the outline becomes mainly indistinguishable to the eye. The drawback of this is that higher resolutions cost more money.

Vectors, on the other hand, are made up of 'line segments' and so provide more limited painting and colouring facilities, but the creation and manipulation of outlines can be achieved more easily. Therefore vector software is used extensively for lay planning and grading, as well as the final stages of embroidery design.

Figure 2.3 illustrates diagramatically the visual differences of lines on a raster based and vector based system. At the moment raster and vector displays are incompatible from a software point of view, being difficult to work together technologically. Sometimes even established CAD users have not been aware of the differences of the two techniques, and have been puzzled as to why, for example, outlines on raster based systems can lose some detail when scaled to a different size.

Operating systems

Every computer has a disk operating system, which essentially consists of a special software program to ensure that the system as a whole operates in a correct and orderly fashion, ensuring the simple listing, saving, recalling and running of programs. It may be seen as a behind-the-scenes 'personal organiser'.

Many personal computers today run an operating system known as MS-DOS which stands for Microsoft's Disk Operating System. The more powerful, sophisticated computers known as workstations run other types of operating systems, such as Unix, providing additional benefits not readily available with a personal computer.

Some personal computers, such as the Apple Macintosh range particularly, hide the operating system from the user by covering it completely with a graphical user interface. For most designers this is desirable, since involvement with MS-DOS can be an intimidating experience – visually it looks like double Dutch! Generally it is not necessary for the designer to become too involved with DOS but knowledge of its existence is useful and aids general understanding by allowing the designer to get more from the system.

Apart from being a command structure, MS-DOS is the software engineer's entrance to accessing the computer, to add or alter software operations. If involvement with DOS is necessary for any reason, the main point to remember is *don't panic*! You will survive, and so will the computer! Essentially the operating procedure is straightforward and logical, and although it does take a little time to understand operations, it can be seen as identical to keeping a looseleaf file of information split into various sections or directories.

System crashes

A colloquial computer term heard every so often is 'the system crashed'. This means that for some reason the software program has jammed or stuck, disabling operations totally. This is quite likely to happen to a CAD user, as the result of a number of different possible causes, for example: selecting an odd sequence of functions; not properly selecting a function; not enough disk space or memory; or occasionally it may be a hardware fault, such as power supply fatigue.

When the system crashes, again *don't panic*! You will not have broken the whole machine but just stalled it, similar to stalling a car. To continue working, the system will have to be restarted, or rebooted as it is known technically.

If the system does crash during work, and the design has not already been saved in the library, that particular piece of work might be lost depending on the particular type of graphics board being used in the machine. Therefore it is important to adopt the habit, when starting to use a design system, of periodically saving the design while working on it, so that if the machine crashes a recent version of the image can be retrieved immediately from files after rebooting, so saving the designer from having to start again.

Scanning

Desktop scanners, as opposed to the larger drum scanners used by the printing industry, are available in a number of different sizes. The

(a)

(b)

Fig. 2.4. Size and visual difference of an image scanned at (a) 75 dpi, (b) 300 dpi.

smallest is an A5 handheld version, A4 is a medium size, and A3 is the largest size for the average budget, in keeping with a PC based system. Naturally, for inputting a wide range of visual imagery a colour scanner is more desirable than black and white, although the latter is perfectly acceptable.

The software enables images to be scanned at various dpi (dots per inch) according to the task being carried out. Currently the general parameters for scanning on a personal computer are 35 dpi minimum, and 400 dpi maximum, with a number of possible variations in between. Any part of an image can be selected for scanning, and it is important to be aware of three main factors:

(1) The process of scanning requires a certain amount of disk space to operate, so the computer's hard disk space should be checked before scanning starts. The higher the resolution selected the more disk space required for scanning.

(2) The particular dpi selected for scanning will govern the resulting size of the image. If an image scanned at 100 dpi is compared with an image scanned at 200 dpi, the higher resolution image will be four times larger in size overall, and more detailed simply because more dots or pixels are used. Therefore if a high quality scan is required, a higher resolution should be selected. Figure 2.4 shows the difference in size and detail of the same image scanned at 75 dpi and 300 dpi.

(3) After scanning, the image will consist of multiple colours irrespective of how many colours there are on the original artwork. To convert the scanned picture to the same number of colours as the original, colour compression software must be used. Some paint programs provide this, some do not. If not, the artwork must be cleaned of all rogue colours by hand which can take many hours of laborious work. Figure 2.5 illustrates the colour differences of a magnified section of artwork before and after scanning, and after cleaning up the image using colour compression software.

Colour

Colour palettes, and the possibilities for manipulating and controlling colour on raster based design systems, are infinite and complex. They result from binary arithmetic, on which digital computing is based. On the higher resolution raster based CAD systems it is possible to access between 262 000 and 16.7 million colours for design use, with between 256 and 1.3 million colours on screen simultaneously, depending on the graphics board and the size of monitor.

These figures are standard and depend on a number of technical parameters. Without going into too much mathematical detail, the particular graphics board used in the system will consist of a particular number of bits-per-pixel. A bit is the smallest unit of binary information stored in the computer, and a group of 8 bits – a BYTE – is capable of storing one of 256 possible functional alternatives.

(a)

(b)

(c)

Fig. 2.5. Magnified section of art work showing colour content (a) original artwork, (b) after scanning, (c) after cleaning up.

   Graphics boards are made to support a number of different bits-per-pixel, all of which are multiples of four. For example:

- 8 bits-per-pixel
- 12 bits-per-pixel
- 16 bits-per-pixel
- 24 bits-per-pixel
- 32 bits-per-pixel

Generally personal computer design systems use graphics boards which are either 8 bit, 24 bit or less commonly 32 bit. How these technicalities control colour, and subsequently affect the designer, can be explained simply.

Design system working in 24 bit mode

Red, green and blue are the primary colours associated with the additive colour process, and as mentioned previously a group of 8 bits allows 256 alternatives. Since every dot or pixel on screen can be addressed separately, working in 24 bit mode essentially means that every dot can have 256 different levels of firstly red, secondly green, and thirdly blue, making a total available palette of 16 777 216 different colours. It should be noted that on a 19 in monitor displaying 1280 × 1024 pixels, only about 1.3 million colours can be seen at once.

Design system working in 8 bit mode

The mathematical restrictions of colour working in 8 bit mode can be confusing for the designer, so only the very basic principles are explained here.

   Although the maximum number of colours is again 16.7 million, only 256 colours can be handled at any one time. The translation of colours from computer to monitor occurs in what is called the look-up table or LUT. On an 8 bit system, each pixel contains a number between 0 and 255. This number points to an entry in the LUT, which in turn gives three values between 0 and 255 for the red, green and blue component of the required colour. Since there are 256 entries in the LUT, each pixel can be defined as any one of 256 × 3 colours, giving a total of 16.7 million.

   How does this affect the designer? Table 2.3 lists the main creative advantages and disadvantages of working in the different modes.

Table 2.3. Advantages and disadvantages of 24 bits *v* 8 bits-per-pixel

	Advantages	Disadvantages
24 bit	Maximum number of colours available.	Unable to flood fill areas of imagery quickly.
	Good for airbrush, wash, shade, tint, softening the edges of a raster image by averaging the intensity of neighbouring pixels, and colour mixing i.e. for creating more subtle visual effects.	Unable to create colourways easily. Disk space can fill up quickly. Loading full screen pictures can be slow without a dedicated hard disk.
	Good at merging complex images.	
	Excellent quality visual results for presentation.	
8 bit	Quick colour manipulation such as flood fill and creating colourways.	Only 256 colours on screen at once.
	Only 256 colours on screen at once (fewer colours on screen at once could be seen as an advantage).	Special functions and features such as airbrushing and merging images are limited or not possible. Sometimes a striped effect occurs when scanning subtly shaded images. Unable to display multiple designs on one screen using different colour palettes for each. Not enough colours.

A further important factor regarding colour is the understanding of the two fundamental colour processes. Obtaining colours by mixing rays of light, as on a computer, is known as the 'additive' colour process, whereas mixing pigments or dyes to obtain colours is known as the 'subtractive' colour process.

Here we have one of the most difficult dilemmas of CAD: it is technologically impossible at this time to reproduce the colours available on a computer on a sheet of paper, and vice versa, because of the fundamental differences between the two colour processes. Much research has been, and continues to be, undertaken in an attempt to overcome this technical difficulty, but a further problem is that it is very easy to adjust the brightness and contrast of the monitor from day to day, thus affecting the colours seen on screen.

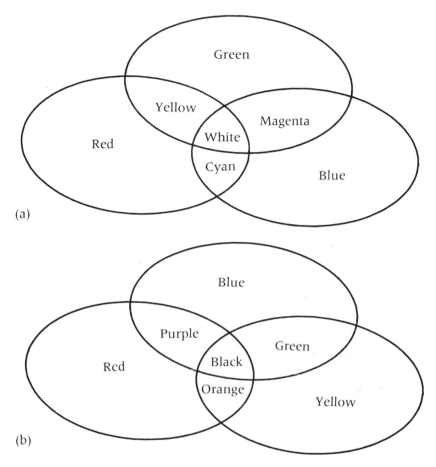

(a)

(b)

Fig. 2.6. Differences and distribution of the (a) additive and (b) subtractive colour process.

Figure 2.6 illustrates the rudimentary differences and distribution of additive and subtractive colours.

Colour printers

A convenient point to consider initially is how to colour match the image on screen so that it can be correctly printed on to the paper. A number of possibilities are available, none of them totally satisfactory:

- Each printer is able to produce a certain number of colours which will vary according to the particular technology. Either the colours can be matched automatically by the computer to the particular printer, or the designer does it by means of a colour book which relates to the colours available.

- Some design systems support specific production colour systems such as Pantone and Scotdic, which provide not only a colour chart but a reference number for each colour. As yet it is not possible to output these colours automatically from any printer.
- Some printers attempt to colour match as accurately as possible without the designer having to resort to controlling the colour. If the colours are simple primaries or brights sometimes the results are acceptable, but it can be rather hit and miss.
- Colours available from the printer will vary with the particular manner in which the dots are printed on to the paper. There are various printing alternatives, known technically as 'dither patterns' and 'microfont matrices', which essentially control the pattern and the number of dots printed. For example, one pixel on screen maps to 4 dots horizontally and vertically on the printer. This is known as a 4 × 4 microfont matrix size. There are various microfont sizes and by altering these it is possible to manipulate the total number of colours a printer is able to produce. The resulting visual effects of imagery printed with different microfont matrices can be a useful aesthetic aid to the designer.

There are a variety of printers on the market today, all operating different processes. These include inkjet, thermal, dot matrix, laser and, more recently, sublimation. Prices range from £600 to £60 000.

Paper surface and size will vary with each printer, being either shiny or matt and ranging generally from A5 to A3. A £60 000 printer can print up to between A1 and A2 in size and is matt.

Library storage

One of the most beneficial aspects of a CAD system is the ability to store designs, images, text or whatever within the library. The saving and retrieval of designs is a simple operation which generally takes a few seconds, depending on the size and complexity of the visual.

As CAD becomes more common in the textile and clothing sectors, companies are beginning to realise the potential of keeping records of design ranges on disk, rather than in cardboard boxes which are left to gather dust in a warehouse. With CAD, designers have at their finger-tips all the resource material required for developing future design ranges.

A software engineer's view

Generally when a new piece of software is to be written, there is a typical procedure followed by the engineer to create the program. (The word 'create' has been used deliberately since software writing is a creative activity.)

Initially the engineer will determine the purpose of the function – What is it supposed to do? This is followed by determining how to present the user interface for the designer so that it works fluently and effectively. At this point the basic options of the function are worked out, followed by the primitive operations to get the function working; for example the menu colours on screen and a simple toolkit which might consist of adding in some numbers or a few questions and answers.

It is then possible to start building the function by looking at the basic operations, for example 'In > Option > Out', and trying out each option of the function one by one. The aim is to check that all options available to the designer integrate well together and provide the most direct manner of achieving the solution.

Ninety per cent of the program takes 10% of the time to write, and the final 10% takes 90% of the time to test and perfect. As with designers, software engineers have their own handwriting which can be identified by other programmers as different methods of arrangement and the amount of attention paid to getting the function or program to operate efficiently.

The visual composition of software code on screen comprises a mixture of letters, symbols and sentences, as shown in Figure 2.7.

From a designer's viewpoint, working closely with a technical team can provide a fascinating insight into software development and can facilitate a more realistic understanding of the technical parameters which govern CAD.

Summary

Once a designer has had the opportunity of working on a CAD system and has sampled the magic, for example, of colouring a design in a fraction of the time it would have taken traditionally, the immediate response is to expect the system to do every task that needs to be done, and as quickly. Unfortunately this is not possible.

This chapter has brought to the attention of CAD users some of the basic parameters of what can and cannot be achieved and the reasons why. In turn it is hoped that designers of the present and the future will be encouraged to become more involved and will take more interest in learning about the basic technicalities of this most exciting design tool.

Many times in the past few years designers have been heard to

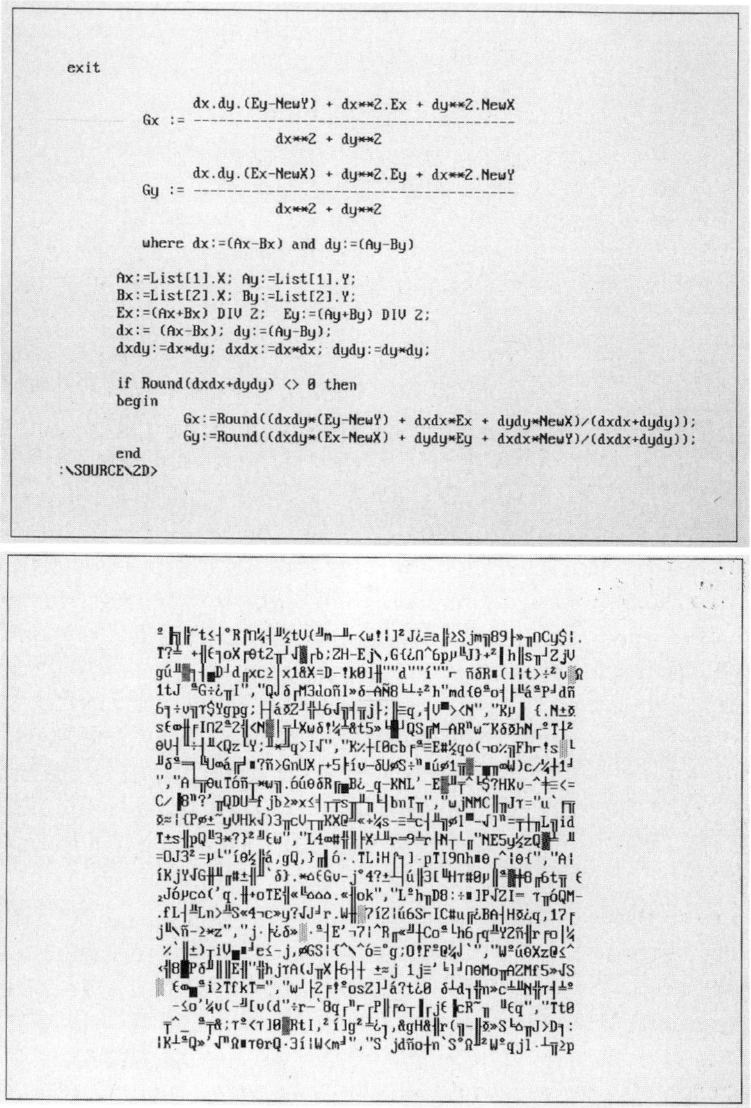

(a)

(b)

Fig. 2.7. The visual appearance of (a) software code, (b) computer trash.

remark, 'I don't want to know anything about computers; I just want it to work without getting involved in the technical side'. This can be understood, but such a view is limiting since with any machine there is a certain amount the user has to know in order to operate it effectively. For instance, a car is a reasonably sophisticated machine which the driver must first learn to operate, before passing a test to indicate a degree of skill and competence. With continued practice it is possible for the driver to fine-tune driving performance, and sub-sequently the driver must learn to maintain the car so that it operates to its full potential.

Naturally a designer does not have to take a test in order to use CAD, but there is a certain amount of learning with regard to the particular computer and software package which can include some technical understanding, but no more so than that of driving and maintaining a car. By so doing the designer is in a much stronger position to gain the real benefits of working with such an advanced tool.

There is also a need for the computer experts, be they research and development or sales based, to listen seriously to the require-ments of the clothing and textile industries, particularly regarding design and production software. All too often in the past the com-puter companies have dictated to designers as to their requirements, without truly understanding design tasks. This inevitably causes con-fusion and frustration to the user since they are being asked to think and operate in an alien manner. It would appear that some computer companies expect designers to adjust their working habits substan-tially to fit in with the software package.

When suggestions have been made by designers for specific func-tions, a regular response from technical departments has been 'Why do you want to do this?', followed by 'It cannot be done'. As a result, all too often, the newly purchased system is left to sit in a room by itself, untouched, since it is not sympathetic to a designer's manner of working.

For the producers and users of CAD technology to push out the barriers and break new ground, both technologically and aesthetically, *both* sectors must become more aware of the other's requirements and technical parameters, rather than each sitting in ivory towers. A more intergrated working relationship than has so far taken place between CAD producer and user, must provide a better foundation for continued computerised development to assist the clothing and textile industries in the future.

Acknowledgement

The author thanks Noble Campion Ltd and Image Data Design Ltd for their assistance with technical advice.

All Registered Trademarks are acknowledged including Microsoft Corporation, Noble Campion Ltd, Apple Computer Ltd, Pantone Inc, Scott-Munsell Colour System.

THE MARKETER

Chapter 3
Marketing CAD/CAM

DOUGLAS AND MARGARET COOPER

Douglas Cooper was educated in South Africa. He spent five years working in clothing manufacture, five years in production and two years in sales. He then entered the family textile machinery business where he worked for many years.

For the past thirteen years he has been involved in the introduction, sales and the servicing of CAD/CAM equipment in the United Kingdom. His experience and knowledge of the early introduction of CAD/CAM into large companies has been gained by his practical involvement in major CAD installations.

The section of this chapter that deals with the introduction of CIM into the workplace has been contributed by Margaret Cooper. It has also been published in the March 1990 issue of *Professional Engineering*.

CAD/CAM systems

The history of CAD/CAM clothing systems is a complex tale centred on the appearance (and disappearance) of various suppliers of CAD/CAM equipment to the garment industry.

It was in the early 1970s that four men in Dallas, Texas, got together and thought about the idea of making markers on a computer. This was the foundation of CAMSCO. At that time operators who made markers manually were having to travel backwards and forwards along long laying-up tables, placing card pattern pieces on paper and drawing round them. If one thinks about the different sizes and pieces involved, the gap between the pieces, the constraints (e.g. nap, flip, tilt, etc.) one can appreciate that it was no easy job. Above all else the marker had to be efficient. i.e. giving the best possible fabric yield.

The ability to computerise the placing of pieces within a given area was not such a difficult task. The real difficulty was that these pieces were odd shapes which contained punch holes, notches, stripe lines, grain lines etc. and these all had to be catered for by the computer system. This problem was solved by electronically tracing the irregular shapes and related information and feeding this data into the computer – a function referred to as digitising, and this worked very well.

There was one other task which these four men from Dallas wanted to achieve and that was the ability to grade via the computer. To grade manually was a long-winded process because new pattern pieces had to be made for each size. It was decided that grade-rule tables should be created. This meant that the X and Y directional co-ordinates for a grade point were assigned a rule number. To generate the same movement for another grade point it would only be necessary to apply the corresponding number. With this in hand they now had the basis for a grading and marker making system. The output of graded pieces, singularly or nested, as well as planned markers, either scaled down or full size, was possible by the use of a plotter made by Gerber, another American company.

Just after the Dallas team set to work, another software house in America acquired the expertise of two of the Dallas programmers and started to develop their own system which they marketed for three or four years under the name of The Hughes AM1 System. Eventually this system was sold to Gerber, who had already established themselves as suppliers of plotters and numerically controlled (NC) cutting equipment.

By this time there were two US companies supplying marking and grading systems. Both established offices in Europe and England (I headed up one of them). While all this had been going on, a Spanish clothing manufacturer had been developing a system for in-house use, but they did not enter the selling arena until the late 1970s or early 1980s. It is interesting to note that all three companies were using Hewlett Packard mini computers as the platform for their software, and the results were good. At this time PCs had not come into their own.

Later in the 1980s a French company, Lectra, started developing their system, so we now had four companies marketing computerised marking and grading. It was not long after this that Gerber bought CAMSCO and founded the Gerber Camsco Organization; so we were back to three companies. Five years later Ron Martell, who had been one of the Dallas four, started his own company, Microdynamics, and brought out a PC based system.

The development of the Assyst system

Around the same time Assyst, a team of four in Germany who had worked for the US companies as well as the Spanish company, were listening to the market. As they were maintaining many systems throughout Europe they had established relationships with many manufacturers. There was a 'hole' in the market place for a pattern design system. Although all the competitive systems suppliers at that time were offering pattern design and/or manipulation facilities on their equipment to varying degrees, none were satisfying the market at large which had an appetite for a pattern design system (PDS) which could successfully be used in a production environment.

Numerous manufacturers discussed this problem with Assyst, who decided to write such a package. The company had a good working knowledge of systems on the market and they were able to note down, in their plans for a new system, the good and bad points of existing systems in the market place and what was needed. In addition, they had at their disposal much more powerful hardware and more sophisticated software development tools to choose from than CAMSCO or Gerber ever had at their outset. They also had the choice of whether to go for a PC based system, as the others in the field were doing, or to go the mini computer route. They chose the Hewlett Packard mini computer route for many reasons.

Their first task was to develop a PDS which could be used in a production environment; secondly, this system had to have the ability to pass data to and from many other computers and devices without interrupting the design operator. To do this a multi-tasking operating environment was specified and although micro computers had limited capabilities in this field (a typical limitation would be a significant reduction in speed during concurrent activities) none could match the speed and power offered by high performance mini computers running under the Unix environment, (bearing in mind that Unix is specifically aimed at multi-user/multi-tasking operations). The PDS was a great success and they have committed extensive development resources into marker making, grading and automatic pattern generation (discussed in more detail later). This is how the Assyst system came into being.

So now we are back to five systems on the market. There are of course one or two more but the accepted big five are the only ones to have made a significant impact on the world market.

Early marketing directions

In examining the CAD/CAM marketing of the last two decades it is necessary to look at the way in which sales were directed. Who made the first purchases and why?

I came to England in the mid 1970s and opened my own office for marketing CAMSCO systems to the clothing industry. I had only one competitor, the Hughes Apparel System, and I think we both entered the UK market at the same time. The European offices of both companies were already open. The first system in the UK was a CAMSCO sold to Ladybird and they wanted it to drive their Gerber cutter. The

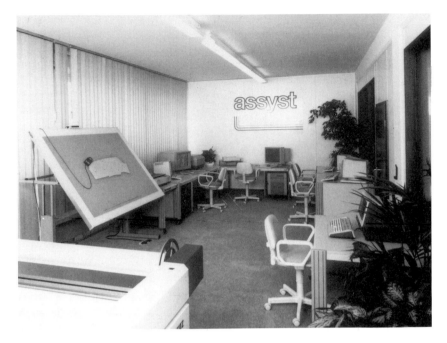

Fig. 3.1. The Assyst CAD system.

second system was sold to a Northern Ireland company making shirts and they bought it to save cloth on the very large orders they received from big retailers. This they achieved by being able to make markers and to know exactly what fabric utilisation they were getting, because the system gave them this information.

As I started to call on customers in the UK I came up against two main problems. The first was the price of a system which started at about £200 000 and meant that this was the most expensive purchase a company had ever made, apart from the building they were housed in (if they owned it). The second problem was that a lot of the customers were supplying the big retail chain groups and were required to submit a sample in each size, say from 8 to 18 for example.

This was not too difficult but when the samples were tried on by the models, in the various sizes, the buyers asked for alterations to be made to the garments. The manufacturer would have to go back to his factory, alter the patterns, remake all the samples and submit them again. In some cases the nested patterns after alterations bore no resemblance to the graded nest he first started out with. A size 12 in one area could be larger than a size 14 etc. I was told on many occasions that if I could get the manufacturer's customer to accept one sample made up and a print out of the nested grade, I would have an immediate system sale.

It was S R Gent who bought the third CAMSCO system in the UK. Their justification was on speed of throughput only; any other benefit would be welcome. It was this company who were the first to submit two samples (12/18) and a nested grade and have it passed for fit. To us, selling systems, this was a great breakthrough. It also had another spin-off. The large retail groups were now telling their suppliers that they should get into this new technology as it would ensure better fit and more accurate patterns. This was wonderful news to us on the marketing side.

Now Gerber took over the Hughes AM1 system and from this they developed the Gerber AM5. It had better software than that of the AM1, the hardware was improved – particularly the screen, and it still used a Hewlett Packard mini computer. By this time they had developed the flat-bed plotters which were not only faster but also did not use the expensive sprocket-fed paper required by the drum plotter.

This was an interesting time from a marketing point of view. A large textile Group made the decision to go into marking and grading systems in a big way. Both Gerber and CAMSCO were asked to quote. We both went in with quotes of about £120 000 per system and we were told that we had to do better than that as the initial order was for about eight systems with more to come. I don't know exactly what went on in the Gerber camp but within CAMSCO UK and CAMSCO Inc. there was great excitement. We were going to get this order. It was obviously the same at Gerber. I cannot remember the exact prices that were quoted back and forth but in the end Gerber won at a greatly reduced price which was between £70 000 and £80 000. The next phase was to be at a higher price, but that order put Gerber fairly and squarely on the UK map. They were also beginning to sell their numerically controlled (NC) cutting systems in the UK – a market which had proved to be the biggest outside the USA.

The Gerber cutter was a boon for the manufacturers who had large capital budgets. Gerber also had worldwide patents on their cutters so they had this segment of the market to themselves. CAMSCO could also drive the Gerber cutter and later all the other makers of CAD/CAM systems could also drive cutters. The marking and grading system was now within reach of a far larger section of the market. The £100 000 barrier had been broken and not long

Size of manufacture   System prices

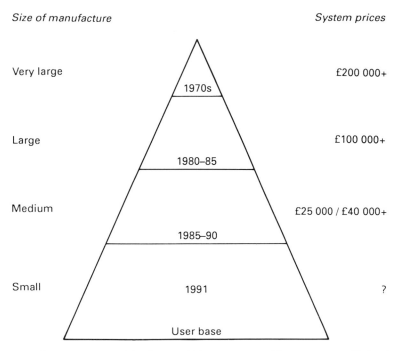

Very large   £200 000+

1970s

Large   £100 000+

1980–85

Medium   £25 000 / £40 000+

1985–90

Small   1991   ?

User base

Fig. 3.2. The price pyramid of CAD/CAM systems. The systems sold in the 1970s and early 1980s are now being replaced; as the price of systems comes down so the user base increases.

afterwards the £75 000 barrier was also broken. Figure 3.2 illustrates the price pyramid.

Current marketing directions

Gerber, who currently operate under the banner of Gerber Garment Technology, have absorbed CAMSCO and have ceased to market the AM1 and AM5 systems and released the PC based Accumark system. Lectra are well established with their own standard system and cutter. Investronica are well established with a PC based system and they also supply cutters. Microdynamics are in the market place with a PC based system. Assyst are also here but with a mini computer based system and this is running on the Unix operating system. All other systems are running under MS–DOS/PC–DOS, with the exception of Lectra who wrote their own operating system.

It was with this advent of PC based systems that the market place changed. Prices are as low as £25 000 up to £40 000 for a base system. One of the main reasons for the low price is that hardware prices have come down and the competition in the market place is very fierce.

Grading and marker making

All the systems can grade pattern pieces with various degrees of sophistication and speed. All systems can make markers. Some vendors even claim to have an automatic marker making package but this is little more than a marketing gimmick at the moment because none of the markers produced are efficient enough for a production environment. They fall short by about 8% to 10% or more. One size costing markers can be achieved with an automatic marking system.

When Assyst selected their hardware from Hewlett Packard, this company had just launched its HP9000/300 Series which had been voted by the engineering world of aerospace, automotive and ship building as the most powerful tool available. This is vindicated by sales of such equipment to the likes of the aerospace industry, Rockwell International, General Motors and many more. It was able to offer connectability to other systems, which meant a buyer of systems could choose different types of system to best suit various applications and have them able to pass information back and forth. The Assyst PDS package was sold to users of existing systems, again mostly CAMSCO, who connected the PDS work station to their existing system and passed over block patterns to Assyst's work station for style creation and grading. Once this was done the graded pieces went back to the existing system, and the markers were made.

Pattern design systems

PDS is widespread in Germany and Italy. In the UK the market is very slow to accept it, with a few notable exceptions, for example S R Gent and Frank Usher; the former uses Investronica, the latter Assyst. Other companies in the UK use PDS for alterations, e.g. trouser lengths or skirt lengths, but not for the total creation of a style from a basic block, except when the style is very simple. I think this is due to the fact that a lot of our UK production is for the large chain groups who buy fewer styles but in large quantities. In Europe you have small orders, larger style choice and more detail in the garments, which means you have to have fast throughput. I predict that this will change in the next few years.

The other new development in the market place of system software is PGS, or pattern generation software. At present the two packages I have seen are from Assyst, called Conex, and from Investronica, called PGS. The following description is a broad overview.

The system has a size table, an alteration table and style listing. There are also up to a hundred questions to answer about various parts of the garment you are making, e.g. the lapel – what width if different from the style you have chosen etc. The system can then create a full set of patterns in all the sizes you have chosen, for the outer fabric, linings and interlinings. Typically 40 sizes can be created in 10 to 20 minutes; this is all the pattern pieces graded (outer, linings and interlinings). This is then transferred to the CAD system from a PC and stored with a style name, piece name and sizes already graded ready for marker making.

Computer integrated manufacturing

The 'buzzword' at the moment is CIM (computer integrated manufacturing). An example of this is the direct transfer of production data to the commercial electronic data processing system for further processing. Any data from any individual system within the factory can be made available to any other computer. This concept is gaining popularity but there is still a long way to go. To implement CIM requires time, money and a lot of nerve. In a lighter context it could be referred to as 'confusion in management'.

Introduction into the workplace

While consideration of the various operational aspects of CAD/CAM systems has been made, the effects of the use of CAD/CAM systems on people should also be addressed. Imagine what goes through a person's mind when management tells them that the tasks they have been performing manually all these years are now going to be done via a computer. Most people are aware that robots are replacing workers on production lines; skilled people worry that they will be made redundant, not only from their employment but also from their present technology.

The modern view of manufacturing industry tends to see people as an irritant, to be neutralised/minimised, not as a resource to be developed. In fact the ideal manufacturing unit is often visualised as being filled with robots and empty of people. The reality is that maximum flexibility and commitment to quality relies on a marriage of these two costly resources.

The recognition of the link between people, organisational management and profitability has led to improved design of equipment and working conditions from the operators' point of view. However, it has not led to them being involved in the more pro-active approach of seeing people and their flexible skills as central to the development of systems, equipment and strategies for managing change.

The great need is for a change in the attitude to change itself. The successful organisation of the future needs to see change as a continuing, welcome and productive state and it needs to institute structures, attitudes and a culture which supports change and the people who are an intrinsic part of the success of such an attitude.

This fundamental change in approach touches every part of the organisation, as people intervene in some way in the planning, decisions and implementation of all the functions. Therefore, 'human factors' become a more comprehensive and interdisciplinary topic than 'ergonomics'.

This poses questions about how to reduce fear and make the right choices about people, equipment and the way forward, how to change attitudes in manufacturing management to the role of people in the generation of profit, and how to encourage shop floor workers to believe they need and have the skills to be pro-active in an advanced manufacturing technology environment. It also prompts questions about the long term education/training of workers both at school and in industry.

Such a far-reaching change will inevitably bring about a period of chaos, where the old attitudes and organisational culture remain but do not support the new needs. The majority of UK manufacturers do not have the luxury of a fully automated, turnkey project, complete with skilled workforce. Neither is this a solution to the problem of managing change if the full range of human resource issues has not been considered. Organisations must accept that people have ability, are willing to take responsibility and will welcome change if they are encouraged to participate in shaping that change.

Identifiable problems

Unfortunately, the need to cope with an existing situation has mitigated against taking a more long-term view. The fact that management is 'too busy firefighting to consider fire prevention' has led to a reactive rather than a pro-active approach.

Within the flexible automated assembly area, this has resulted in counter productive actions and attitudes, including:

- Concentrating on ways of automating the assembly of existing products rather than having automation in mind at the design stage.
- Using the wrong criteria for judging success in implementing new technology. These go as far as asking, 'Does it work?', 'Can the workforce use it?' and 'Will there be pay back within a given period?', but fall short of questioning the more long-term benefits to developing business options, such as 'Does it offer the scope to cope with continuing change in product range and volume?'.
- Creating islands of automation which like welds in an exhaust pipe show up, or even produce leaks elsewhere in the system, resulting in loss of vital information and expertise exchange, necessary for the future.
- Creating a climate of fear, hostility and stress as the need for various skills seems to disappear with the advent of new technology.
- Gearing pay to greater specialisation and thus building in more rigidity.

Strategies for implementing change

The change in attitude and policy necessary within industry to counter these problems and give the human factors issue higher profile, starts in the brief of top management. It covers issues ranging from timing and planning of on-going change, through attention to recruitment, training, counselling, career path, hierarchical structures and reward issues, to the recognition and development of transferable skills within the workforce, and the communication and utilisation of information between individuals and departments, and the effect on the design, choice and implementation of new technology.

THE CONSULTANT

Chapter 4
Consultancy in CAD for Clothing and Textiles

PHIL WIGHT

Phil Wight obtained his degree in Electrical and Electronic Engineering at the City University, London. He started his career as an Electronic Engineer and became involved with the clothing industry when he joined Courtaulds, developing computer controlled knitting machines. This was his introduction to the world of computers and he joined CAMSCO when they opened their UK offices in the mid 1970s. He installed the first CAMSCO systems in the UK and became Technical Director of the UK company. On the take-over of CAMSCO by Gerber, he remained as Technical Director of a new company CCS, who became agents for the Investronica System.

In 1986 he formed his own company, Productive Management Systems, to develop software packages for the clothing industry. He took a short break to set up and run the UK branch of Investronica. Once this was established he returned to PMS as a consultant to companies purchasing CAD/CAM technology. He is presently consultant with some of the main clothing manufacturers in the UK.

The need for a consultant

The role of the consultant in the field of CAD/CAM technology has only recently become apparent and necessary to the garment manufacturer. In the past CAD/CAM technology was restricted to grading and marking systems and was available from a limited number of suppliers. The basic CAD system offered three main functions:

(1) *Pattern input* – the digitising of card patterns into a computer system.
(2) *Grading* – the creation of X,Y co-ordinates to generate additional sizes.
(3) *Marking* – the creation of a lay plan via a graphic work station.

The choice of system was restricted to two main overseas suppliers. With the introduction of the micro-based computer in the early 1980s came the opportunity for other companies to emerge as suppliers of CAD systems. This led to over five additional suppliers offering CAD technology to the garment industry. Of course with the increase in suppliers came competition and the great price war.

At the end of the 1970s a basic CAD system with one display, digitiser and plotter, cost over £100 000. At the end of the 1980s the cost of the same basic system had fallen dramatically to around £40 000.

Competition led to cheaper systems for the garment manufacturer but caused the system supplier to develop less expensive hardware in order to reduce their system selling price.

At the end of the 1980s this price war reached a trough and it became impossible to continue the downward trend in system price. However, the competitive spirit still remained and the system suppliers had to look elsewhere to gain the edge. This has led to the software war and the suppliers are now making available all sorts of software packages to entice the customer to buy their system.

We now have 'buzzwords' floating around the industry, such as CIM (computer integrated manufacturing) and PGS (pattern generation systems). The concept of a CAD system utilised only for grading and marker making is replaced with the CAD/CAM concept of a common data base with a totally integrated manufacturing philosophy linking manufacturers' mainframe computers to control production units, resulting in real time data capture of work in progress. And if this is not transparently clear to the reader it could be that the appointment of a consultant is overdue.

What can the consultant offer?

With the introduction of more comprehensive software packages, the decision on the purchase of a CAD/CAM system is no longer based mainly on the price. The potential buyer now has to consider all the new facilities and programs and to evaluate the effectiveness of them as an essential part of the continued viability of his business.

The present trend of introducing a totally integrated manufacturing concept (CIM) using a CAD/CAM system from garment design through pattern development, production and finally dispatch, can leave a potential user completely bemused as to how he can maximise his profitability by the use of a particular CAD/CAM system.

Whether a totally integrated CAD/CAM system can practically be achieved within a garment manufacturer's company at the present time can be comprehensibly debated. A better philosophy to follow would be a step by step method, whereby the introduction of CAD/CAM technology within a company is done over a period of time, being introduced in key areas on a co-ordinated and tightly structured basis, beginning with grading/marking, then design and order processing, and finally manufacturing.

Grading and marker making departments have long accepted CAD/CAM technology as standard. Apart from a few advances in these fields – the most noticeable being automatic marker generation for costing markers (not sufficiently advanced for automatic production markers) – there have been no major developments in these areas.

Most large garment manufacturers have some form of CAD/CAM grading and marking system in use. However, computerised cutting has evolved rapidly since the market was opened for other suppliers to sell these cutters. There is no longer a monopoly in cutters, and as with CAD systems the competition has brought prices down. More companies are looking at introducing this technology.

However, the introduction of computerised cutting into the normal cutting room requires a great deal more consideration and control than may at first sight seem necessary. This is where a consultant can be of most benefit as it is where really significant savings can be achieved. Most cutting room staff do not have any CAD/CAM experience and a major retraining program is required. Obtaining the optimum link between the CAD department and the cutting room is vital for problem-free transfer of data between these operations. A high degree of co-ordinated control is required to avoid incorrect cutting of styles which results in high re-cut cost and fabric wastage.

The consultant can play a vital role in three major areas:

Pre-installation

The consultant will look at the customer's present working methods and in particular at the area where CAD/CAM would be beneficial. Beginning in the design department he will consider the use of concept design systems, and the method of producing new designs and offering these for approval, to customers. Is there a need for a 'sketching system', where first concept design can be created on a graphics display and different fabrics/colours overlaid on to the original sketch to produce a hard copy print out of a new garment design? Will customers accept these designs rather than the traditional sample garments? Or could this be a half-way measure to reduce the number of sample garments?

Presently there are few companies using these sketching systems as an effective replacement for actual garment selection, mainly because present technology has not evolved within the customer selection departments to accept 'designs by floppy'. The main reason is that it is difficult for the selector to obtain a 'feel' for a garment when it is only represented on paper. The cost of these systems is very high at present and the quality of print that can be achieved is not of an acceptable level. However, there are increasing signs that this technology is gradually being accepted by customers and we will certainly see an increase in the number of garment manufacturers buying these sketching systems in the future.

Next comes pattern creation. Most companies still create their hard card patterns by manual methods because present pattern technicians have been trained manually with card patterns and the technology has only recently been available to achieve pattern creation by computer. With the pattern design system (PDS) and more recently pattern generation system (PGS) now available on most CAD/CAM systems, the computerised skills of the manual pattern technician can be utilised more effectively and accurately. These facilities can be used to replace all present methods of manual pattern creation. The benefits of using a CAD system for pattern creation will result in more consistent and accurate patterns, as well as faster responses to design changes.

There is however a reluctance by the pattern technicians who have been trained in the traditional ways, to accept this philosophy. This creates a hurdle that requires a great deal of 'educating' or high pressure selling. The good news is that more and more colleges of further education have now gone down this path of computerised pattern creation, and the present pattern technicians entering the industry are trained or at least experienced in the field of computerised pattern design systems.

System survey

A consultant will evaluate present systems on the market and their suitability to the customer's requirements. With at least six major suppliers of CAD/CAM systems now, this is essential. All systems will provide adequate grading and marking functions, but their suitability to fit in with the present methods of grading and marking departments and future development, must be considered. The grading method of the system, the size ranges available and the present identification protocol used on pieces and markers, must be looked at. Is there any link to mainframe computers and production control systems? What additional software features are available that will improve the overall performance of the company?

For a small company interested in grading and marking only the choice of system could be heavily influenced by price, as all grading and marking systems are fairly compatible. The consultant will evaluate each system by visiting the supplier with his client for an initial preview of the system. From these visits he will select two or three systems for a more detailed investigation. Based on the set of parameters drawn up during pre-installation, final selection begins. Certain styles may be selected for trials and these will be carried out on each system selected. The support and back-up services of each supplier will also be taken into consideration.

With advances in computer technology, the choice of hardware used by the supplier will certainly have to be taken into consideration. It is vital that the hardware is up to date and that as far as possible the supplier will not be changing hardware within a short period, leaving the customer with an outdated machine soon after it is installed.

It is not only a matter of deciding which system to purchase, but of how the system be fully utilised to improve the overall performance of the CAD/CAM departments.

Post-installation

The consultant oversees the successful integration of the selected system within the company's organisation, including the implementation of new working procedures to optimise the performance of CAD/CAM technology.

Any main CAD/CAM supplier will be at your beck and call before a decision on the purchase of a system. Once a system has been installed and the initial training period has expired, so does the support and advice from some suppliers. This, however, is the most crucial phase of the introduction of a CAD system. Training may have been carried out on how to use the system in terms of inputting patterns and marker making, but the operation and integration of these procedures within the company becomes a stumbling block. New paperwork to control the flow of work from department to department needs to be created. Other departments connected with the CAD system need to be educated as to what can be achieved from a computerised system, and how they can obtain the best use of this technology.

The introduction of a CAD/CAM system within a company is far more extensive than most companies realise. Generally most CAD/CAM systems are only being utilised to about 60% of their true potential, and in some cases less.

It is after system installation that the failure or success of the project will be decided. All CAD/CAM systems work, but many take much longer to reach the 60% efficiency than is necessary. The use of a consultant can not only achieve this target more speedily and effectively, but can also increase this to 70% or 80%.

The creation of the proper paperwork, not of any fixed format but that which is best suited to the existing methods of workflow in the company, forms the building blocks of a better controlled and managed system. Standard checks can be introduced to avoid costly errors.

The consultant acts as a guiding hand to lead the operators down the shortest and most efficient paths. He is not there to run the system and act as system manager, which is often assumed. He is the adviser to the staff in the appropriate departments, who are the people that must do the work.

The consultant can be important to the garment manufacturer about to embark on the challenging journey of purchasing a CAD/CAM system. Regardless of which system is selected, proper guidance in its implementation within the organisation can be very beneficial to the company. The worry of successfully installing a CAD/CAM system can be transferred to the consultant, leaving the director responsible to embark on yet another journey with only the occasional glance back to see how progress is coming on.

The consultant, as the temporary navigator of the ship, can now guide the crew successfully to their destination in the shortest possible time and with the minimum 'walking the plank' situations. The question for the consultant is what flag will he have flying on the main mast? Will it be French, Spanish, German or American? Could it even be British?

Can the consultant be truly independent?

When deciding which system to recommend to his client, the consultant may be coming on board with a certain flag already in his pocket.

An evaluation of any commodities involves a thorough investigation of the pros and cons. As a result of the findings, a decision is made on which comes out best. It can be assumed that further investigations will always result in one item being selected as the best, and therefore earmarked as the item to recommend.

Although the evaluation may have been based on a set of standard specifications, any investigation must include the suitability of that product to different individuals' needs. A certain product may be best according to the standard criteria, but when individual requirements are taken into account another may be more suitable.

Technology is continually advancing and the system suppliers are striving to maintain this trend. The product of yesterday is seldom the same as today's or tomorrow's. So it is with CAD/CAM systems. Because of the complexity of these systems and the different packages available, it is not possible to evaluate a system purely on set parameters. Parameters have to be devised to evaluate the CAD/CAM system for the particular client. This is achieved during the pre-installation consultancy period. Then during the system selection period the consultant evaluates the present systems on the market and compares them to these parameters.

So the consultant always comes on board with at least five flags in his pocket, and as the journey begins he one by one tosses the flags overboard until there is only one left. This flag he proudly hoists on to the main mast, and yet another and even more challenging journey begins.

The future of CAD/CAM in the clothing industry is an exciting prospect. CAD has remained dormant for too long. The time is ripe for real advances in this technology. New operating systems, networking the processing power of computers together, will lead to more complex systems, and the philosophy of a totally computer integrated management system may at last be on its way.

THE CAD BUREAU

Chapter 5
Making the Grade

TONY WALSH

Tony Walsh graduated from the University of Newcastle upon Tyne in Mechanical Engineering. He later studied at Hollings College, Manchester, gaining a post graduate Diploma in Clothing Management and Technology. He worked for Hepworth Tailoring from 1972, becoming responsible for the installation and management of one of the first CAD systems in the UK clothing industry in 1975. He was involved in the development of this system for made to measure. He helped to set up and run Com Plan Technology Limited as a CAD Bureau for the clothing industry, becoming Managing Director in 1985.

The CAD bureau for the clothing industry

Back in the early days of 1981 when Com Plan Technology was established and CAD bureaux were in their infancy in the UK clothing industry, customers were easily impressed by the technology. For many it was their first real exposure to the use of computers for grading and lay planning and they viewed it with a mixture of awe and fear. If we were to keep those customers we quickly had to lower their expectations of what the technology could offer them and allay their fears by showing them that the CAD system was only a tool – in the hands of an experienced clothing technician a very powerful tool, but useless without the skills of the designer, the grader and the lay planner. The mystique of the 'black box' had to be removed, together with the idea that you pushed a button and it all happened.

Nowhere was this more relevant than in lay planning, where many believed that simply because computers were being used material must be saved. Today our customers are more sophisticated and less easily impressed. For some, coming to a bureau is the first step on the road to having their own in-house CAD system, and the independent bureau can show them if and how CAD can help them and the true cost.

For most, their interest is in the end product and it matters little to them whether we use 'light pen' or 'ink pen' to achieve it. The bureau's primary concern must also be with the end product, and it must use the equipment, and above all the staff, that will enable it to achieve a standard of quality higher than the customer would reach themselves. For what would be acceptable from an in-house source becomes unacceptable when 'we are paying good money for it'. In this respect the bureau is the most severe test of the CAD system and the ability of the staff to run it. It must achieve a consistently high standard, be able to work on ladies fashions, wetsuits, bras and cassocks all at the same time, deliver to the clothing industry standard (i.e. yesterday) and, at least as far as the independent bureau is concerned, make a profit.

Design

Design can often be the first stage in the process, but first the term must be defined. The designer can be the person who produces the style sketches or creates the first pattern, and occasionally is both. I like to differentiate between the two functions by calling the first styling and the second pattern design. Styling has no place in our bureau since we believe it would compromise our position. By this I mean that we work on styles from a wide spectrum of eminent customers, and even though it would never be our intention to copy we could not fail to be influenced by what we had seen. Therefore to avoid the suggestion of plagiarism and maintain our professional integrity, we limit our services to pattern design.

I do, however, hold a strong opinion on the relevance of CAD to styling. CAD styling systems are neatly defined by the generic term 'sketch pad' systems, though companies selling these systems prefer to use more elaborate language. It is generally supposed that these sophisticated drawing and colouring machines will stimulate the creativity of the stylists and enable them to produce more styles more quickly. Perhaps this is so, but a competent stylist can visualise a style and efficiently transfer it to paper without the need for this technology, and maybe this is another example of computers being used because they can be rather than because they need to be.

There is a principle of computer applications here that is relevant throughout CAD, and that is that the more a piece of data is used, the cheaper it becomes. The problem with sketch pad systems is that the sketch is the only end product. These systems operate independently, are not linked to the main CAD system and cannot transfer data to it. Work is being done on software that will convert a three dimensional style concept into a two dimensional pattern, but a practical solution is a long way off and then we would be asking stylists to produce engineered drawings rather than sketches. CAD systems could be used as a sales tool to show the buyer that there are other options, but all this adds further weight to my argument that sketch pad systems have no place in a production orientated CAD bureau.

Pattern creation

The style concept comes from the customer, usually in the form of a sketch, and it is the bureau's job to translate that into a working first pattern. This is done by referring to our own library of tried and tested basic blocks, but often we find that we have to draft a block from scratch. Our pattern design software is one of the most advanced available, but still we find that while a new pattern can be constructed on a blank screen, it is quicker to draft by hand and then input it to the computer. Under some circumstances this could be different, for example with a large product range over a narrow band of product types, and a design technician totally dedicated to the application of CAD to pattern construction, i.e. he or she is doing it all day, everyday. In essence, CAD pattern construction is a 'use or lose' type of skill and therefore only finds a place in the largest design rooms, where its potential for standard pattern manipulations done quickly and accurately can be fully exploited. Strangely it is often this aspect of CAD software that (after price) is used to determine which system is purchased, and for most it will be the software which is least used.

When a block pattern has been established on the computer system the situation is very different, for the basic structure can be manipulated, dissected and reconstituted to create the desired styles, with the speed and accuracy expected of computers. We do this extensively in our bureau and will do so even more as we learn new applications for this aspect of CAD. The principle of block design is vital to the successful application of CAD in pattern design, meaning that many styles can be created from few blocks. The stylists must be encouraged to view their styles in this way, while not compromising their creative freedom. The fact that the bureau will charge less for pattern design from an existing block than creating a new block introduces a discipline that will help to concentrate the mind of the stylist.

Grading

The next stage in the bureau process is grading. Contrary to popular belief this can be a slow and painful process in CAD because time and skill are required to establish the grading data on the system. The computer grader must input the pattern to the computer, interpret the size chart, build the rules on the computer, apply those rules, and plot out and check the grade. The manual grader will move and mark the pattern to the size chart, checking as he goes.

It is when the grading data is established that the speed of computers can be exploited, by reusing the grading rules on similar styles. However, it is not an automatic process and can never be taken for granted. Good grading skills are needed to check the output from the CAD system and to manipulate the data to achieve perfection. After grading we invariably submit a full size nest to our customer for approval because, while the grade is technically correct, there will be other ways of doing it and the customer must agree with the method used. If grading using CAD is to be cost effective it is important that, as far as possible, the grading system is standardised so that grade data can be re-used. This will rarely be absolute since even slight changes in line or seam placement may require a change to the grade rules. But now it is more a case of modifying rather than creating grading systems.

Fortunately, in the vast majority of cases, our advice is accepted. Indeed I can recall only one customer who was insistent that each style in his range was unique and should be graded differently. Our advice was that in those circumstances CAD was of no help to him. Our attitude to our customers in this, as in all aspects of our services, is that the customer is always right, even when he is wrong, but we reserve the right to tell him we think he is wrong.

Once a grade has been approved by the customer the style may proceed to pattern production or lay planning and occasionally both. The only additional pieces of information needed for pattern production are the sizes in the grade which are to be produced in card form, and the quality and colour (or colours) of the card required. Most orders are then completed and despatched within 24 hours.

We may also be asked to produce a pattern with different stretch or shrinkage factors from those allowed for in the original pattern. We simply need to know the increase or decrease in the warp and weft allowance and that change can be made automatically and a new pattern produced. The changes will be applied proportionately throughout the whole pattern so that the balance and fit of the original pattern are maintained.

Lay planning

Lay planning is a more complex issue and full details must be known of the cutting situation in which the lay plans are to be used. There are the physical constraints such as the usable cloth width, the table space available and the order ratio; and practical constraints like the cutting equipment and the skill of the cutting staff. A bureau must know and understand all the factors that will influence the cutting of the order, and must produce lay plans that will work in the customer's chosen cutting room. All lay planning, whether CAD based or manual, is a compromise between the efficiency of the lay (i.e. how tight it is) and how easy it is to cut. The art of lay planning is in balancing these two conflicting interests.

There is a popular misconception among those who have not used CAD, or at least not for production lay planning, that the lay planning process in CAD is automatic, meaning that you press a button and the computer unassisted produces the perfect lay plan. The truth is somewhat different. Lay planning is essentially a creative process requiring good spacial awareness, and not everyone has the ability to do it. It is not a jigsaw puzzle with a perfect solution in which each piece has only one possible position; it is a compromise between material and cutting efficiencies in which each piece has an infinite number of possible positions and orientations. Computers are particularly inept at dealing with processes in which there is a creative element, and the trial and error approach is limited by the possible variations. Sophisticated algorithmic programs have now been developed by most system manufacturers to approximate the skill of the human lay planner, and that is just what they do with predictable results.

Automatic lay planning will produce lays requiring 2% to 5% more fabric, with poor cutting characteristics. But progress is being made in this area of development and no one can predict how quickly the technology will take us there. When it does I will be the first in line to buy, for I would love to be able to guarantee to every customer that I can save them material. Of course automatics can be used for rough costings, where all that is required is an approximation of the material usage, but customers are not interested in approximations.

So for now and the foreseeable future our only option is interactive marker making, i.e. using man and machine. The only difference between what we are doing and what our customers are doing is that we have skilled lay planners sat in comfortable chairs moving patterns around electronically, while they have skilled lay planners running around tables with pieces of cardboard. A lay planning service gives customers time, for a CAD system enables lay plans to be produced quickly at a consistently high level of material utilisation. How much material is saved depends on how good or bad the customer's lay planners are and how long he is prepared to let them work on each lay plan.

Where orders are small, garments are simple and fabric is cheap, CAD lay planning is a total overkill and not cost effective. Bureaux must be the first to recognise this and advise customers accordingly.

The end product of lay planning is usually marker making, i.e. producing full size copies of the lay plans. Where a customer has in-house diozo type copying facilities all we need to supply is one master copy of each marker. For the remainder, copies can be ordered as and when required and are normally despatched within 24 hours.

For customers who are factoring the product through cut, make and trim in the UK or abroad, a costing marker is required; therefore only a material rating figure, possibly with a miniature copy marker, is needed. Armed with the bureau's engineered production patterns and accurate material usage figure, the customer can negotiate a realistic price with his supplier. Also, because the customer owns the data he has paid to have developed, he can quickly source the product elsewhere should problems arise, or can have a parallel supplier with the confidence that at least in terms of fit and fabric cost the product will be the same.

Confidentiality and data ownership

Title to the data put and stored on bureau computer systems lies with the customer that paid for it to be put there. Data cannot be transferred to, or used for, the benefit of a third party without the specific written instructions of the first party – the customer. This has occasionally meant refusing data on styles to very large companies and organisations who we know own those styles, but they were brought to us for processing by the supplier and it is the supplier who pays us to create the data. Invariably this problem is resolved by the supplier transferring the data to his customer, but the principle is inviolable.

Apart from the ownership of the data, security is also very important. To those companies who invest heavily in the development of patterns, those fragile pieces of card can represent the life blood of the company. When fire, flood or some other disaster has struck one of our customers, we have been able to replace patterns within hours or days.

Servicing the customer

The essence of a successful CAD bureau in the clothing industry is service. As an independent bureau unencumbered by association with, or ownership by, any system supplier, college, local authority or garment manufacturer, we are able to dedicate ourselves to the service of our customers. Maintaining a reputation for quality and service, in our case, takes over 20 staff, almost all of whom are highly skilled clothing technicians, designers, graders or lay planners, they operate a shift system to ensure that services are available to customers from 7am to 9pm on week days throughout the year, closing only for bank holidays.

The CAD system enables us to fully utilise our skills for the benefit of the customers. We recruit and train skilled clothing technicians, not computer operators. CAD operation can be learned quickly, but the skills of the clothing technician can take a lifetime to master.

The CAD bureau's customers are anybody involved with patterns. I am constantly surprised and gratified by the range of products and size of companies that come to us: the one-person design consultant who will use our services to enhance his or her own; the small design companies with two or three people who are factoring their production and need technical support in pattern design, sizing and grading and material costings; the small manufacturers, where our services will release the designer (or owner) to do what he or she wants to do, i.e. design; the medium size companies who can no longer find or afford the in-house skills, yet must maintain and improve quality of fit and the efficiency of material usage; the large multi-site company where consistency and control are essential; and the CAD user who needs support in times of machine or people breakdown, or help over seasonal peaks.

For all these customers the first questions are: how much and when – in that order. Companies that do not have in-house resources against which to compare bureau charges can find that the prices for this professional service are little more than they would pay their plumber and a lot less than they would pay their accountant. Where comparisons can be made the company only has to consider that a bureau does not require sick or holiday pay and is only there when needed, to conclude that the services can be cost effective.

As to 'when', the conversation goes something like this:

Bureau   'When do you want it?'
Customer 'Yesterday will do, but the day before would be better.'
Bureau   'When do you need it?'
Customer 'Tomorrow.'
Bureau   'When does it go into production?'
Customer 'Next month.'
Bureau   'OK, let's agree a schedule.'

And so we agree a delivery schedule, and in a properly scheduled production plan there is no waiting time. But despite fax machines, modem links and overnight delivery services, it has to be admitted that the bureau cannot react as fast as the in-house CAD system, and it is logistics more than cost that will encourage the larger customers to buy their own CAD system. It is not the bureau's job to promote CAD, *per se*; indeed, because we have to fulfil the promises we make, we show CAD 'warts and all', but that is inevitable if we are playing our proper role. Hence it is more with pride than regret that we see customers installing and using their own equipment, having evaluated their needs and set their standards by the services we provided.

The future of the CAD bureau

Judging by our own recent investments in buildings and equipment, the CAD bureau faces an optimistic future. While CAD systems are much cheaper than they used to be and in real terms, at least, will continue to fall in price, buying a piece of equipment is not the whole story. I would guess that at least 80% of those that buy systems find they need to increase their budgets after the first year by 30% for capital, and 50% for labour and other revenue items. Companies that need to control their expenditure will continue to look to bureaux to provide CAD services at a budgeted cost.

CAD system manufacturers are now providing programs that will allow their systems to interface with competitors' equipment, thus enabling data transfer between different systems. Therefore I see the bureau playing an increasing role in supporting CAD users. But the most important factor is the continuing decline of sound technical skills in the industry. The bureau will deliver those professional skills using the latest CAD technology and based on a deep understanding of customer needs and the meaning of the word service.

THE USERS

Chapter 6
The Impact of Computer Graphics on Clothing Design

CLIVE WALTER

After graduating from Brunel University, Clive Walter worked in the defence and electronic industries. He joined Marks and Spencer twenty two years ago, where he has specialised in manufacturing technologies which improve the effectiveness of the company's supply base. He is a Chartered Engineer, and a Fellow of the Institution of Mechanical Engineers, the Institution of Production Engineers and the Institute of Quality Assurance.

Customer requirements

What is it that attracts a customer to a garment in a store? The initial impact will be its colour and the design on the fabric, be it the stripe on a shirt, the print on a blouse, the lace on a slip or the jacquard on a jumper. These, together with its shape, give an immediate visual impression – an instinctive feeling of like or dislike. There are other factors too, such as how the fabric feels when handled, how well the garment is made, how comfortable it is and how well it will wear. These add up to give a perception of the garment quality. The major purpose of the clothing and textile industry is to provide garments that will sell and give satisfaction to discerning customers.

Use of CAD

CAD, with its ability to simulate these visual impressions, is currently creating much excitement in the industry. Why? How is CAD being used? What changes are occurring? What is the significance of these changes? How will CAD develop? Interesting questions – the answers to which will emerge from consideration of how a garment is developed from the initial design to its planned production.

Before doing so, however, it is worth considering the historical perspective of CAD, which is not new to the industry.

CAD in fabric design

Some of the earliest applications of CAD occurred in fabric production, when mechanical programming by chains and steels was replaced by relays, actuators and other electronically controllable mechanical devices. In knitting and sock machines it is the selection and movement of needles and beds that is programmed, whereas in weaving it is the selection of warp threads. On CAD systems any sequence of selection to produce the required design can be simulated as a grid on a monitor. Each square on the grid is given a colour corresponding to a knitted loop or woven thread. Computers are thus able to give a visual image of the knitted jacquard or a striped or checked fabric. Both colour and sequence are easily changed as the design process is refined. Once complete, the electronic information is transferred to control the mechanism of the production machines.

CAD in clothing design

The clothing industry has also made good use of CAD. It happened when an alternative to the manual method of using a reciprocating straight knife was developed by Gerber. It was the numerically controlled, plunge knife, automatic cutter. This required the definition of the digital information which describes the shape of the pattern pieces, together with the sequence in which they should be cut.

Computer technology came to the rescue. The shapes of cardboard pattern pieces are given X and Y co-ordinates by a digitiser and entered into a computer. This enables pattern shapes to be displayed on a monitor. Grading, or how each pattern shape changes to allow for different sizes, is automatically achieved. For this to happen the displacement for each significant point on the pattern edge is determined by a set of 'grade rules'.

Planning how the patterns should be nested together in a lay plan to ensure maximum usage of fabric, has become an interactive routine between an operator and computer screen. All the pattern pieces required for a given cut ratio are displayed in miniature, and these are manipulated, rotated and fitted together between two lines which relate to the fabric width. The finished lay plan forms the basic information required to describe the path of the automatic fabric cutter. This information is passed to the mechanisms which control the path of the cutter and other machine functions.

Pattern modification systems have been developed which enable basic pattern shapes to be altered for different style and construction features. Computer technology is used in the whole of the process from pattern design to the control of the cutting machine.

Historical perspective

The historical perspective, therefore, is that CAD has developed from the production requirement and progressed to the technical aspects of design. In many instances CAD has stayed within the production environment, and in this environment designs are offered which can be produced easily and economically. In principle this is commendable but there is a danger that production considerations may restrict design.

Computer colour graphics

The advent of computer colour graphics is beginning to change the perspective by giving designers an innovative tool which is challenging their expertise. The scope of CAD has been extended to include the whole spectrum from design initiation and decision making through to technical design, with the subsequent link to production plant and machinery.

The garment design process

Garment design, like all design, does not exist in a vacuum; it has to respond to the perceived needs of customers in the marketplace. Necessity is said to be the mother of invention; it is equally true of garment design. An understanding of customer needs is of paramount importance, particularly where garments are sold to a mass market.

The retailer is well placed to define precisely those customer needs. Major retailers nowadays operate worldwide. They have knowledge of selling patterns in stores, and they keep to date with fashion trends and fabric, yarn and component developments. They also keep aware of what is new and what is being sold in the major capitals of the world. This enables them to forecast and give clear directional guidance to their fabric and garment suppliers on predicted customer needs in the season ahead.

The garment manufacturers' designers also keep abreast of fashion trends, receive the directional guidance, and have a knowledge of the production requirements of their manufacturing plants. From this they can offer designs which they consider satisfy the perceived customer need.

All this sounds very straightforward. In reality, it is an iterative process, particularly in a fast changing fashion scene, with design ideas proposed, discussed and modified. Fabric, colour, fabric design, lace and trimmings, silhouette and cost all need to be determined before a decision to place a contract is made. Even then the iterative process continues as the garment is developed, and the technical aspects of fit, grading, construction and garment performance are considered.

It is said that design is 10% inspiration and 90% perspiration. The perspiration is the iterative nature of design, the exploration of different options in order to achieve a coincidence between the designer's creativity and the customer's perceived need, at an acceptable cost.

To sum up, the design process passes through four stages:

(1) *Design initiation stage*, in which the marketplace customer's perceived needs are defined in terms of colour, silhouette, style and fabric design.
(2) *Design concept stage*, when many design options are explored and result in design offers which satisfy the defined criteria of customer needs.
(3) *Decision making process*, where design offers are considered, ranges are developed and decisions to purchase are made.
(4) *Technical design stage*, where the design offer is refined to precisely satisfy the fit, construction, garment performance and production requirements.

Creating visual images

Computer colour graphic systems provide a powerful tool for both the retailer and the garment designer, particularly during the first two stages of design. They are able to determine colour, simulate fabrics both printed and woven, simulate components such as lace and embroidery, and map these on to drawn silhouettes and styles to give a realistic representation of drape. Thus they create a visual image of a garment, its colour, fabric design and shape – just the attributes that initially attract a customer when they enter a store.

Significance of computer graphics

The significance and benefits of computer graphics during the design initiation and design concept stages can be considered as:

Better communication

A picture is worth a thousand words. A visual image that bears a close resemblance to the finished product enhances the communication between designers and buyers, between sales and marketing, between buyers and stores and within departments and organisations.

Greater responsiveness

Decisions on garment offers can be made closer to the proposed launch date. Also it gives the ability to make changes rapidly once the sales pattern within a range is known; the garment offer can be changed to more truly reflect what is and is not selling. It is responsive to immediate customer needs.

More considered design offer

The designer is able to explore quickly, inexpensively and thoroughly the design options, be it colour, fabric design or shape. The chance of achieving a sample garment right first time and acceptable is increased. The result can be a substantial reduction in sample costs.

With more traditional methods the time between design concept and seeing a garment or fabric samples can become extended, particularly where change is requested. This can lead to a compromise decision when time runs out, with neither designer nor buyer completely satisfied with the design offer.

Production innovation

Designers are able to be more creative and offer more complex prints and graphic designs. This attracts customers with new ideas, and gives freshness and appeal to the range of garments on offer.

Widening role of garment design

By responding directly to the market need, garment designers are becoming more involved in fabric and component design. In selling a design concept they have also made a contribution to the marketing aspects, how a garment might be packaged, how product information is presented and how garments might look in a store environment. They are becoming the focus of the total design activity.

Technical challenges

This changing role of design and use of computer graphics is however presenting challenges that need to be resolved.

Remote communication

The electronic communication of pictures of high resolution with true colour representation will be needed at speed and at an affordable cost. Such interactive communication could be needed between the garment designer and the retailer, between the garment designer and the fabric or component designer, and between the garment designer and the production source, in all cases both locally and internationally. Development continues on fast transmission links and data suppression techniques.

Connectivity

Connectivity or the transfer of structured design information throughout the whole product design and development chain, is required if the benefits of responsiveness and reduced costs are to be achieved. For example, a fabric print created in a garment design department should be capable of electronic transfer to a fabric printer. Colour separations determined on computer should be capable of transfer to screen production systems such as laser engravers. Colour co-ordinates should be capable of transfer to dye prediction and colour kitchens to achieve the desired colour in production. The information flow should be two-way with each stage communicating the detailed needs of each process in the chain.

It is vital to ensure that the visual images created at the design stage – 'What you see' – are faithfully reproduced in production – 'What you get'.

Colour communication

This is the most important technical issue. A consistent true colour regime is desirable, in which the colour seen on different monitors and printers, responding to the same colour co-ordinates, is the same both within a system and between systems. The ability to dye fabrics using the same co-ordinates to achieve an acceptable colour match, is also an objective.

Computer aided design department

A design department, in making a design offer, is faced with two requirements: the ideas which make up the concept must respond to the market needs; and how much will it cost? The concept requirement will be addressed with the aid of computer graphics, but what of the costs requirement? For this the essential computer systems from technical design will be required, together with knowledge contained in computer databases.

Pattern design systems which estimate fabric costs, and databases which contain manufacturing methods, production costs and fabric and trimmings costs will all need to be integrated within the design environment. The design department has to simulate production right from the design concept stage.

Management of such a CAD department requires personnel with skills necessary not only to motivate creative designers, but also to control sophisticated computer-based equipment. The department will need to be staffed by designers who not only have knowledge of garment production, but also of fabric, components and possibly packaging production. The requirement for training will increase.

Design and market led production

At the beginning of this chapter the question was asked, 'Why is computer aided design currently creating much excitement in the industry?' The answer is the application of computer graphics within both the marketing and design environments. This is giving effective communication of consumer needs, and a creative, speedy response to those needs.

The role of the clothing design department has been enhanced as they provide a design response that co-ordinates fabric, packaging and component design, with close links to the sources of production. The designers are being supported by high tech computer systems and databases. They are encouraged to be more creative and bring fresh ideas to the marketplace to attract customers. The industry is being design and market-led with design challenging production.

Chapter 7
CAD in the 'Real World': Using CAD Clothing/Textile Systems in Industry

ROZ DAVIES

After graduating in Clothing Management from the London College of Fashion, Roz Davies started her career as an Industrial Engineer at Reldan Ltd where she practised fundamental Production Management techniques in clothing manufacture. She moved to the London Design Studio of Slimma Casualwear as a production engineer using her knowledge at the 'front end' of the business in the costing and development of new products.

An extension of this role was pursued when she moved to Coutaulds Leisurewear and carried out special projects in the manufacturing divisions before setting up the position of Technical Manager in the London Design Studio. This position has involved the management and development of computer aided design, product costings, total quality and the sample machine room.

Introduction

The phrase CAD in the 'real world' emphasises the day to day pro-ductivity requirements that a CAD tool will have to cope with in an ever demanding industrial environment. There is an excitement and frustration in taking theory into practice and continually improving our processes of design and product development to give us a com-petitive edge.

As Technical Manager of Courtaulds Leisurewear Design Studio, my role has developed into looking at and introducing new methods of working in the design, product development and manufacturing process. Earlier experience in clothing management and industrial engineering, and later experience in quality and design management, has meant an increasing interest in CAD for the last two and a half years. Only now do I feel that I have a clear understanding of what is required to take the industry positively through the 1990s.

My view will very much reflect the mass production and large retail chain store side of the business, but I believe every supplier in the clothing and textile industry will be looking to achieve excellence in:

- design
- quality
- delivery
- price

Understanding the total CAD offer

Business vision

One of the most important aspects of assessing CAD equipment is getting the business to decide on its overall vision of the future. This vision should not just be general statements of annual turnover and shareholders' return on investment; it should also include strategies on how this is going to be achieved. The clothing industry is too clever at blaming the weather or trends in fashion to avoid the issue of looking into the future rather than just the next few months. We also suffer from our traditional view of the regular three year cycle – good year, mediocre year, bad year, etc. – which we believe will happen whatever plans for change we put into action. We must alter this approach.

The successful consideration of CAD investment will be dependent on the business qualifying its objectives for the future, supporting this with a willingness to change, and specifying financial commitment. These are high demands but I believe that this is the only way of managing a successful long term future.

Once the objectives are in place, there is a structure round which to plan the CAD strategy and take advantage of development and innovation to ensure competitive edge. This technology can revolutionise a business and we must make sure we are on the side that wins!

Who should be looking?

This always seems to be a difficult issue as when computers first came into the industry they were certainly not user friendly to the skilled marker maker, pattern grader or cutting room manager. In the last ten years attitudes and computers have changed enormously, but as users we have become more demanding. Because of this it is important to achieve a project team with a balance of knowledge, expertise and seniority:

Applications expert

Someone who understands all aspects of the design and product development is needed. They must want to change the process and have the ability to sell new ideas and put them into practice. Being controversial and innovative is a distinct advantage. It is this person who should lead the project.

Computer expert

The fast growing development of PC technology, communications and connectivity means that in-house or consultancy support is still needed. As needs become more sophisticated investment in the best tools for each job will be wanted. These might not all come from the same supplier.

Business director

At the end of the day financial support will be needed to put the investment proposal into action. To achieve this a business director must be involved, to understand the opportunities that this type of technology can give the business and champion these views in the boardroom.

For final decision making a broader business involvement will be necessary.

What is available?

To examine what is available, it is essential to know something about the product design activities involved in CAD. These are:

(1) Design
(2) Illustration
(3) Pattern Design
(4) Product Cost
(5) Sample Cutting
(6) Sample Making
(7) Product Specification
(8) Marker Making

It is now possible to apply CAD technology to all these areas apart from sample making, and even that process would be improved if CAD were used in the other areas.

2D Graphic Design

A computer tool with graphic capabilities allows the user to scan in or create on screen many types of images, and then manipulate them with the use of various facilities. The quality, capability and prices vary enormously in this technology. It has proved to be a valuable asset to design, illustration and selection. Issues, important to the industry are cost, colour, high image resolution, greater sensitivity to the designer and links in the supply chain.

Pattern design

A computer tool allows the user to scan, digitise in or create pattern blocks on screen, apply grades and redesign pattern pieces where necessary. There are several of these systems available with similar functions and price ranges. Some of them have embraced the future worldwide reduction in pattern technology skills, and some have not. Ease of use, speed of use and communications will be fundamental issues for the future in this area.

The possibilities of designing and pattern cutting in 3D are not as far away as we think!

Costing systems

A computer tool allows quick and easy access to standard minute, trim and fabric databases for the calculation of a full product cost. As we gradually become more professional in business the need for accurate product costings and the monitoring of cost fluctuations become paramount.

Progress in this area seems to have been slow, which has always been a surprise to me. Maybe the industry does not want to know the truth! Accurate data collection, maintenance, ease of use and inter-pretation into the design environment are important aspects.

Sample cutting

An automatic cutting tool is driven by a pattern design system with the ability to cut single ply fabric fast.

The process of cutting and making samples is very expensive. The aim with 2D graphic design is to reduce this, but we must also be aware that growth in product ranges and other developments will also affect sample making. Therefore it must be made more cost effective, with quicker response time and greater accuracy. The capability to cut single ply without paper patterns and without using valuable manpower time and skill, can only be an asset.

Production specification

A computer allows a graphic image to be displayed with a product description and a specification of make-up in one facility. Today some part of the manufacturing facility is normally abroad, which has resulted in the need to bring back the use of production specification. This will be the amalgamation of information already compiled, so it will need to be linked to all the other systems and probably customised for company's own needs.

Marker making

A computer tool enables pattern pieces to be placed on to a fabric lay. This is the area which has seen the greatest CAD application so far and most of us rely on it totally. It might need up-dating to take advantage of its new ease of use, cheaper maintenance, increased speed and connectivity.

Will it really work?

One of the problems of visiting computer shows, CAD/CAM suppliers' showrooms and the like, is the difficulty of telling the good from the bad, the real from the contrived. The best solution is to take your own work, on which you can see demonstrations in real time. An even better solution is to have the system on trial in your own premises, which would mean you could use it as your first stage of the learning curve.

Talking to other users can be useful; they will normally tell you the truth. But never forget that CAD/CAM suppliers are always trying to sell you something. It is very important to look at maintenance agreements, company growth and profitability, and the company's view on future developments.

What are the developments?

A strong approach to developments is an essential requirement for CAD technology. Gauging the time span of computer software and hardware issues is difficult but a logical and well planned programme should provide some protection from this. It is important for users to drive the suppliers' research and development teams in the right direction to ensure practical solutions to problems. We must also share our visions of the future so they can maintain a lead on our progress. I have already mentioned the areas in which I feel existing equipment could be improved, but perhaps more collaboration between CAD suppliers, the clothing and textile industry and education could enhance innovative thought. At present computer integrated manufacture seems to be the name of the game, with gradual development into the retail business and the supply chain.

Encouraging investment in CAD

Proposing CAD investment can be one of the most challenging problems. There are no easy solutions; enthusiasm and dedication are essential, and sometimes aggressive behaviour might be necessary!

The world of product design is often seen as being artistic, emotive, unpredictable and of course uncontrollable. This view can be solely due to historical and traditional behaviour patterns. We must now realise that with the introduction of technology we have to look at this environment in a new light. We need to consider the costs of product design while maintaining an atmosphere of creativity and innovation.

The key issues for encouraging CAD investment are:

(1) *Education* This is two-fold, educating the business about product design and CAD equipment.
(2) *Costs* Establishing true costs of present methods of working, with particular emphasis on lead times.
(3) *Payback* Establishing a new approach to payback calculations involving hard and soft benefits.

Each CAD investment will have its own characteristics but it is normally the hard benefits that are easier to quantify, although the soft benefits are more powerful.

Hard benefits

- *Speed* Offering the customer a change in print design or pattern construction in minutes rather than days.
- *Accuracy* Removing silly human errors from pattern making and using consistent information data bases.
- *Productivity* Providing a tool to increase productivity by 100% or 200%.
- *Communication* Systems with communication links for quick response and elimination of repeated work.

- *Information* New easy information like pattern stitching measurements for thread calculation and so on.

Soft benefits

- *Quality design service*
- *Informed sales service*
- *Quality product design*
- *Manufacturing flexibility*

Application of CAD in Courtaulds

One of the advantages of working for a large organisation like Courtaulds Textiles plc is that there is always some involvement at senior management level in the development of new technology applicable to our business. On this occasion the liaison link had been established with Computer Design Inc (CDI), an expert software house in America who were developing at that time 2D and 3D design systems for the apparel industry. It became possible, with the co-operation of CDI and the hardware suppliers, to install this equipment at one of Courtaulds Clothings' larger design studios.

The equipment consisted of:

Fig. 7.1. Courtaulds studio.

Fig. 7.2. Courtaulds design work.

- 1 Silicon graphic work station with 2D concept design software.
- 1 PC work station with 2DPC concept design software.
- 1 Howtech scanner.
- 1 Seiko D-Scan thermal printer.
- Ethernet cable to network the configuration.

This is a 2D graphic design tool to assist design, sales and marketing and visual communications.

The businesses to benefit from this opportunity were Courtaulds Leisurewear and Childrenswear with their interest in print design as well as garment design. Introducing new techniques and technologies into a creative environment was an ambitious challenge, particularly when there was no one to follow. The first stages were very basic: finding space, operator manpower, technical support from Courtaulds Information Services and myself as project manager. The next stage was training for the operators in America, establishing methods of working, measures of evaluation and acceptance into the business.

Training

We assumed that to operate a computer in the design environment we needed practical people, so we selected two experienced pattern cutters to train as operators. They went on a two week training course during which they were taught all aspects of the software. Once back in the working environment we immediately set to work to produce valuable services to our design departments. To become an expert full-time user the learning curve was around 3 to 4 months.

Methods of working

To ensure computer work was not lost, disciplines of filing procedures and administration had to be introduced. Once these were established, finding work that had been carried out months before became possible. The next area was setting the colour palettes of the season. Great care was taken to produce good quality colour palettes, which immediately have an effect on the quality of computer graphic design work. If we wanted to show our print designs on real garments, we would also have to organise a professional photographic session. We would make white samples in the correct fabric type and have quality photographs taken so we could ensure the highest standard of computer image.

Measures of evaluation

This was a major contribution on which the success or failure of the trial would be decided. The process was via a questionnaire measuring the:

- Image colour
- Image clarity
- Speed of response
- Accuracy to designer's brief
- Clarity of design brief

There was also an area for general comments. It was here that we began to pick up comments like 'I would not have attempted this without CAD', or 'I could not have done this without CAD'.

The evaluation took place over three months so we had plenty of details from which to analyse the appropriateness of CAD to our business. The result was positive and we wanted the equipment as an on-going facility in our design studio. The financial issue was a lot harder to illustrate and I must thank the business leaders for supporting the gamble with this 'leading-edge' technology. I would like to point out that many of our competitors have followed our lead.

Acceptance by the business

As the installation was initiated by a trial it took some time for the business to accept that the technology belonged to them. It took many talks, demonstrations and presentations to educate ourselves, and of course our customers, about the benefits of having such a tool. This education process is continual as new people become involved in the business.

Two and a half years on

The design and sales function could not 'survive' without it. Our method of working has evolved and I believe we are the only 2D graphic design users that have around 15 designers capable of using the technology, and we are training more every day. With designer users we have discovered new requirements for the system and a sensitive bit-pad and pen with many types of drawing tools is becoming a fundamental need. Quality of output is also a big issue and once we have sorted these areas out the scope will be almost unrestricted.

It has been exciting to see the general acceptance of the facility, which is used to illustrate about 60% of our prints and most of our sketch presentation boards. The interest in using it as a designers' tool has varied from 'really keen' to 'if I have to', the latter being a minority of about one out of twenty.

I now feel quite happy about introducing any new technology into the design studio because they all have an understanding of the trials and tribulations you get at the beginning, and the reward of getting the tool to do the job for you and improve your own way of working.

Improvement has been made in communications across the supply-chain with support from technology links.

Courtaulds support of CAD continues with investments at St. Pancras Way in:

- Concept II Ormus Fashion – for creative CAD graphics
- GGT Accumark – for concept pattern design
- Canon Laser Copier 300 – a must for any design studio.

A competitive future with CAD

We have to analyse the business we are in and identify possible

So the future could look like this:

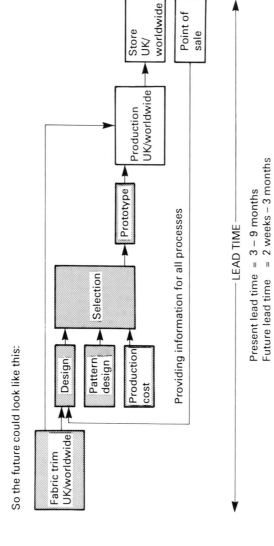

Shaded area indicates where CAD could be used.

Fig. 7.3. Use of CAD in the supply chain.

solutions, in order to achieve excellence in:

- design
- quality
- delivery
- price

Our final customer is now becoming more informed, more sophisticated and more aware of his/her purchasing power and selection. We have to ensure we provide that 'value added' product that they will choose above others. In addition to the requirements above, we will need to offer quick response.

Quick response

We have now reached the time when we as clothing manufacturers have to respond directly to the behaviour of our final customer and use this as information to help drive our business forward. To do this we must use technology in our processes and in our links to the other processes in the supply chain (Fig. 7.3).

This approach is already being keenly pursued by European and North American clothing manufacturers and we are in a position where we need to catch up. Setting up teams of experts across the supply-chain processes, so we can develop common goals and objectives with logical and practical investment proposals and installations, will lead to a successful future.

It will be the 'best users of CAD' supporting a 'value added' quality product with total flexibility that will have the competitive edge.

Chapter 8
Practical Utilisation of CAD Systems in the Preparation, Creation and Processing of Designs for Textile Printing

PETR ŠÍPEK

Petr Šípek was educated at a technical institute for the textile industry in Dvůr Králové in Czechoslovakia. He worked in the economics department of Tiba Ltd before transferring to the department of technical development. Here he selected new techniques and technology for Tiba's factories. He worked on the CAD/CAM system Response 220 from 1980–86 but then returned to technical development to specialise in CAD systems for textile printing.

Introduction

The 1970s saw a rapid and massive introduction of computer technology into the textile industry. A whole range of new and efficient equipment appeared in textile printing, allowing an untraditional approach to the preparation, creation and processing of designs and their subsequent application in the printing media.

The necessity of reacting fast to changes in fashion trends and meeting ever-growing competition made various textile manufacturers apply CAD/CAM systems in textile printing. Unlike today, there were no 'low cost' CAD systems available then; with their strong hardware they took up a lot of room (e.g. systems supplied by Scitex, Hell etc.). For some big textile manufacturers active in textile printing – our company being one of them – the Response system by Scitex seemed to be the most convenient for a variety of reasons:

(1) The final product comes out in the form of film strips (black and white transparency) with the respective colour separation of the design processed.
(2) The system is capable of producing film strips for all printing techniques currently used by textile manufacturers – flat printing, cylinder film printing with both galvanic and varnish screens and cylinder printing/photo gravure.
(3) The high resolution capability of the system is necessary above all for cylinder printing (40 dots/mm).
(4) In later versions such as Response 280 there is the possibility of using various interfaces, e.g. for a laser engraver, which make exposure of films unnecessary.

While this equipment also enables the manufacturer to create his own designs, most companies use it mainly for processing, adjusting and modifying the designs supplied by their clients or originating in the manufacturer's own design department or bought elsewhere.

The present configuration of the Response 280 system operating within Tiba can be seen in Figure 8.1.

With the exception of designs created directly through the system, it is the 12 colour rotation super scanner that forms the input into the system (a black and white plotter-scanner can also be used). This is where pieces of artwork in formats of up to 900 × 1000 mm are scanned, with the time of scanning depending on the design's size and resolution. When using the super scanner, colours are calibrated manually; each colour can be calibrated several times and the system will then calculate the average value of the respective shade. The trimming itself, as well as editing, is carried out on a CDC (colour design console) equipped with a colour monitor, terminal, functional box and an electronic pen with a tablet.

The system has a rich software and its 280 version even makes it possible to program the functions in advance, according to the design's character. A further important advantage is its ability to supply, as the final product, film strips with a hexagon (for cylinder film printing with a galvanic screen) or hazure (cylinder printing), enabling a calculated link-up to the respective screen's or cylinder's circumference. On the other hand, it falls behind the latest CAD systems in creative potential.

The introduction of this system has substantially reduced the time required to process a design. However it should be stressed that a high quality of artwork is essential in view of its limited colour resolution capability. Our company commonly makes use of this equipment as a CAM facility.

The company's production programme

Our production range concentrates on textiles with well-proven raw material composition and treatment that ensure the best possible practical features and require only a minimum care. The collection of designs prepared by the Tiba design studio must hold its ground in severe international competition. Our general collection comprises approximately 3500 designs in six to seven colour variations, and approximately 1750 designs are replaced by new ones every year.

Tiba ranks among the biggest manufacturers in Czechoslovakia who have printing on fabrics as their main activity, although spinning

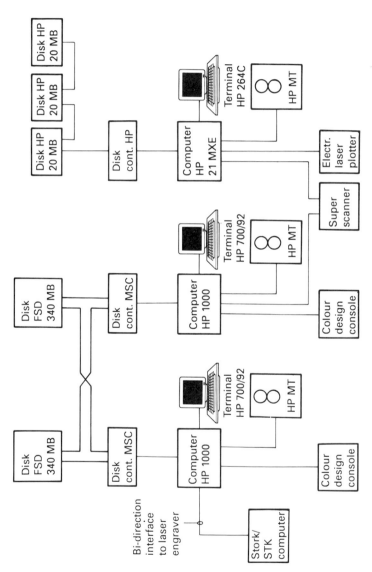

Fig. 8.1. Configuration of the Response system 280/22C in Tiba.

and weaving mills also form an integral part of the company. Tens of millions of metres of printed dress and decorative fabrics, knitwear, bed-linen and other products with designs according to the latest fashion pass through Tiba's gates every year.

The Response equipment has significantly enhanced our competitiveness but, being used in three shifts for technical processing of designs, it leaves no room for creative activity. It was for this reason that the company opted for CAD systems on personal computers. The final decision about the type of equipment to be introduced was, of course, preceded by a thorough and relatively lengthy selection process.

A user's view of what the system should be like

A CAD system for textile printing should enable the creation of the studio's own designs, and the processing of other artwork such as designs on paper, colour hard copy or artwork on fabric.

Input modules

Scanning

This should include the possibility of scanning both colour and black and white artwork in different sizes. It is also important that the scanner has a high resolution capability of up to 300 dpi (dots per inch).

Drawing

The software should enable the user to create the whole design on the screen. The drawing should be carried out with the help of a stylus; using a mouse is less convenient for a designer. The drawing software must comprise a great variety of options: lines of different thickness, vertical and horizontal lines, easy creation of geometric structures, the ability to manipulate the individual parts of a motif within a design and the filling in of various surfaces with different colours, brush effects etc.

Service modules

Correction

For correcting a scanned design, a function for enlarging and scaling down both vertically and horizontally is needed. This enables designs smaller than the original artwork to be processed, e.g. to make a colour hard copy reduced in size and enlarge it subsequently to the original artwork's size.

Colour reduction

In some cases the number of colours in the artwork exceeds the colour capacity of the printing machines, making it necessary to reduce the number of colours. The equipment should enable both automatic and manual reduction.

Colour separation

It is necessary to create a multitude of variations from a finished design and to interchange and combine various colours. This requires the system to be able to produce individual colour separations and to provide storage for their easy re-use.

Colour palette

For successful colour manipulation the user should have easy access to the existing colour palette, but also a facility for creating a colour palette individually. The creation of colour shades must be as simple as possible.

It should also be possible to attach a modern CAD system to a spectrophotometer capable of precisely measuring a design's colour values (essential for printing recipes).

Separations set

From the individual colour separations or their combinations the system should be able to produce a separation recording that could subsequently be used in production machines (laser engraver, film plotter, printer etc.).

Output modules

Colour printer

The printer should be capable of printing out whole designs and their colour variations as well as the individual colour separations. It should also allow the user to print only parts of a given design for checking purposes. Further, the user should be free to choose between a thermo-transfer and an ink-jet type of printer with the highest possible resolution regardless of format.

Production machines

The output for production machines should correspond with the form used in the production equipment, i.e. the same data format and the same input.

Many contemporary CAD systems enable the creation of high-quality designs within a very short time, but they lack linkage to CAM systems. Thus the feasibility of their link-up, on-line or off-line, with systems currently used in the textile industry such as laser engravers (Stork-STK, ZED) or the equipment supplied by Scitex, Hell or other manufacturers, as well as with equipment for the production of jacquard cards, must be a major consideration for any producer of textiles. As an alternative it is possible to fit out this equipment with a corresponding output, facilitating further rapid processing of a design executed by a CAD system (Calcomp Electrostatic plotter, Stork X-cell jet printer, Linotronic etc.).

Another important condition for practical use of CAD systems for textile printing is their resolution capability and their capacity for processing large repeats. For a manufacturer of printed textiles processing a large number of designs supplied from outside, the Desitex V system made by Textile Computer Systems seems to be the ideal solution. We decided to use it in the following configuration.

Design system CPU

Compaq 286 TE complete with monitor and keyboard.
320 Mbyte Winchester, 1.44 Mbyte Floppy and 40 Mbyte tape streamer, clock speed 12 MHz.
C-Graf 16/32C controller.
Digitizing tablet 34 × 48 in.
Colour monitor Mitsubishi model HA 3905.
Laser engraver interface Stork-STK 2000.
Scanner input – Sharp digital colour scanner, single CCD sensor, RGB colour separation, maximum scan area 11 × 17 inches.
Printer output – Mitsubishi G 650 thermal printer.

Work station CPU

Compaq 286 TE complete with monitor and keyboard.
320 Mbyte Winchester, 1.44 Mbyte Floppy and 40 Mbyte tape streamer, clock speed 12 MHz.
Laser engraver interface Stork-STK 2000.
Printer output Mitsubishi G 650 thermal printer.

General notes

Data relating to dye recipes can be printed out from design data, i.e. a database relating to design colours and dye recipes can be built into customers' requirements.

Separation film data from films scanned in on the Stork-STK 2000 laser engraver can be entered into the Desitex V and edited as on the Stork graphics editing unit.

TCS can supply a printer and software to enable designs scanned in on the STK 2000 to be re-assembled, coloured and printed out from the STK 2000 independently of the Desitex V.

The streamer output from the Desitex V for the STK 2000 can be used directly to drive the new Stork X-cell ink jet printer and the Dioden Plotter separation film plotter.

The Desitex V equipment may be seen as a typical example of contemporary CAD systems (Fig. 8.2). It was bought by Tiba mainly for creative purposes, i.e. for creating our own designs. The system pro-

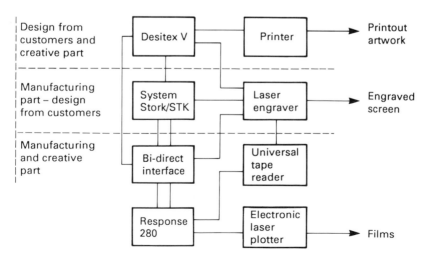

Fig. 8.2. Configuration of Desitex V equipment in Tiba.

vides a high resolution capability (500 dpi) and a high capacity of 12 000 × 12 000 pixels, but above all the designs modelled or processed by it can subsequently be engraved by the Stork-STK 2000 laser engraver without any further operations. Its creative ability far exceeds that of the Response 280 equipment with the type of software we are using or that of the MCD system made by Stork-STK which will be mentioned later. This is hardly surprising however, as they are both primarily CAM systems used mainly for handling designs and not for creating them. From the user's viewpoint the following advantages of the Desitex system are apparent:

- CAD system is totally free of any keyboard use – you need to train your designers to operate a computer if a keyboard is used.
- All operations are controlled through a stylus – no need to learn to draw with a mouse or cross hair.
- Menu and design on one screen simultaneously – a two screen system requires frequent movement of the head to view one screen or the other.
- Confirmation needed on important functions – a day's work can be lost because of one forgetful slip when the system does not use confirmations.
- Designer friendly terminology – no need to learn the differences between 'exit' and 'quit' and other computer jargon.
- Designed specifically for the textile industry with the help of designers – not a system originally designed for other purposes and then adapted to textiles.
- All creative and manipulative operations are effective when designing in repeats e.g. copy/mirror/move/draw etc. – not some work in draw mode only.
- Printing or scanning can be carried out at the same time as designing with no slowing down of either process, and no add-on work stations are needed for these tasks.
- 16 levels of zoom – compared with a limited number of zoom levels.
- Zoom and scroll can be used during a copy or similar function to enable accurate selection and positioning of motifs anywhere on the design at any zoom level – compared with manipulation only on screen.
- Full feature 'undraw' facility which remembers the history of the design and can 'undraw' it sequentially at any time to any earlier state – compared with no 'undraw' or availability only on 'fill' or the very last operation.

- Full function print-out queue which can make use of inconvenient working hours.
- Interface for the Stork-STK 2000 laser engraver – no in-between operation needed.
- Scanning from artwork on fabric possible – no need to redraw the design from fabric on to paper.

The Tiba way of using the Desitex V system

In the spite of its great creative capacity the equipment is also being employed for flexibile processing of artwork on fabric or paper in any form (photocopies etc.) supplied by clients, especially when a very short delivery time is required. We employ it this way because the system uses a high-quality flat scanner in DIN A3 format, provided with excellent software and capable of distinguishing 16 million colour shades. We learned by experience that for processing a large majority of designs a 166 dpi resolution is sufficient. This resolution proved to be most convenient for the subsequent processing by the Stork-STK 2000 laser engraver. A rich menu makes it easy to correct adjustment of the scanner's parameters for each particular design type, as well as to correct calibration of colours. In my opinion up to 70% of the time needed for complete processing of a design within the system can be influenced by the degree of mastering the scanner's operation. The actual scanning can be preceded by the so-called 'initial scan', usually followed by the selection of the desired colours in the final scanning.

After the scanning (designs larger than 11 × 17 in require scanning in several stages), the final retouch and – if need be – editing are carried out, depending on the state of the artwork and its technical level. The system is equipped with an impressive range of functions for design manipulation, retouching, colour manipulation, repeating, changes of design size and creative functions such as unlimited line thickness, wide range of airbrushes – for introducing those difficult random stipples and textures, rectangles, boxes, disks, circles etc. – as brush or shape, copy brush – drawing with a motif or pattern in the brush and more.

The retouching and editing procedure nowadays takes up to 80% of the design processing time. These operations are usually followed by a specimen print-out for checking purposes, effected by a Mitsubishi G 650 thermal printer, and if required by the creation of colour variations, also with the possibility of a specimen print-out. For the formation of colour variations the colour range of the printer instead of the screen, is normally used. This is because we still lack a program that would make it possible to calibrate the printer with the monitor. Then the separation sets – in our case for the laser engraver – are created, but this has to be preceded by the 'Stork rescale' operation that adjusts the design's size to that of the screen on to which it is to be transferred. The majority of the separations are recorded on the work station, so saving design system time which can then be used for the proper processing of designs.

Until recently the Co-ordination Committee on Multilateral Export Controls (COCOM) embargo forced us to use streamer tape cartridges which considerably increased the time needed for recording the separations. When the embargoed technologies became available we decided to use instead the optical discs common with most CAD systems. The fact that streamer tapes are not 100% reliable and that we also used them for storing the designs made this change all the more pressing. There is no doubt that the use of streamer tapes has been the weakest part of our system.

The possibility of creating shades derived from the individual basic colours is one of the system's important virtues, with a direct influence on the final printed product. For each colour the system can produce from 11 tones for the laser engraver and 19 tones for the photogravure. When using a laser engraver a screen of the 125 or 150 mesh Stork H type must be used and the laser's forward shift must be set to 50 microns to suppress the undesirable 'moire' effect. The possibility of forming half-tones will significantly enhance our company's competitiveness because up to now the limited colour capacity of our cylinder film printing machines has made it difficult for us to follow the latest fashion trends with their multi-coloured designs. The half-tone technology removes this handicap, and other CAD equipment owners among textile manufacturers will surely decide to make use of it.

Our company has put into use yet more CAD equipment, namely the Graphik system made by STK Kufstein, supplementing the Stork-STK 2000 laser engraver.

The program's servicing is carried out by means of a built-in menu which means that through a digitiser a function is required and the processed separation can be corrected by the program until the function is changed. The graphic system makes it possible to correct and retouch the scanned colour separations. Missing contours can be filled in and their thickness adjusted. The menu is placed in the lower part of the screen and the colour screen enables up to 8 colour separations to be processed. The choice of the respective place in a repeat is carried out by means of a displayed rectangle, the work itself by means of a cursor. The scanned colour separations can be completed by adding colours at will. This system's maximum size of working window is 50 × 50 mm. The software equipment provides a fast change of function, the carrying out of various enlargements or reductions, and the adjustment of repeat size etc. The graphic station as well as the laser work in an off-line system. As a transfer medium we use 40 Mbyte streamer tape. The graphic system consists of:

- 1 graphic card for the colour monitor;
- 1 colour monitor;
- 1 graphic table (digitiser);
- 1 mouse or stylus.

The b/w scanner's computer is used as a CPU here. The basic Stork-STK system's configuration looks as follows (Fig. 8.3):

Black and white scanner TS 87.
CPU – Phoenix 286 plus monitor and streamer tape.
14 in colour monitor for recording and scanning check-up.
Kennedy type universal tape reader.
Stork-STK 2000 laser engraver with CPU Phoenix 286 streamer tape.

We proceed mostly by scanning the individual colour separations one by one, using the graphic system only for minor corrections and completion. However, the design preparation involves a relatively high proportion of manual work. This is why the use of the graphic system is limited mainly to processing artwork that is not suited for processing by the other systems.

We know from experience that not all designs can be fully processed by CAD equipment. There will always be some client-supplied artwork for which it will not be possible, but we aim to use CAD for the largest possible proportion of the work. This also makes us consider the introduction of a Stork-STK MCD (manual computer design) system, which in my opinion is particularly suitable for combining the actual manual work with a computer support unit.

The basic idea behind the MCD equipment is similar to that of a laser engraver graphic station. The system is integrated with a big light table and all the equipment is used as Stork-STK's production system input. On the light table a contour is taken off manually and then transferred into a graphic system with the help of a TS 87 scanner. All further manipulation with the design (retouching,

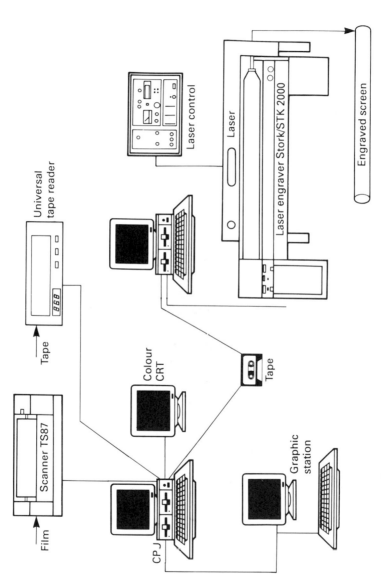

Fig. 8.3. Configuration of the Stork-STK 2000 system in Tiba.

colouring the contours, filling the areas, the drop etc.) is similar to handling any graphic system.

The equipment has significantly simplified the manual scanning procedure and has made it faster while its price is much lower compared with other CAD systems. The MCD also makes it possible to create geometric designs. Its software is being continously improved and upgraded and the system's way of functioning follows trends prevalent in today's world.

The ability to make use of all available methods and their combinations (manual scanning, repro camera, dioden plotter etc.) is a typical feature of the STK's approach; remember that the STK company itself is a major screen manufacturer. We tested the equipment by processing a comparatively difficult design (brush water-colour). We managed to complete the design in a very short time by combining the manual scanning of the contour with further processing on the STK's MCD system.

Having scanned the contour we proceeded to make a b/w watercolour which was then transferred to magenta screen film and with the help of a repro camera to b/w film. The contour and the b/w screen film were scanned by a TS 87 scanner. For the rest of the procedure the CAD system was used, with the colours put into the contour as the last step. Then followed the separation. The whole procedure took us approximately 8 hours.

In our opinion this type of equipment is likely to fully replace the manual scanning in the foreseeable future. We consider it particularly useful in the actual technical preparation of designs for subsequent processing by a laser engraver or a dioden plotter (for flat screens). It is, in fact, CAD/CAM equipment with its final product in the form of technically completed artwork or, more frequently, of colour separations (turned out by DP 88) or input data for the Stork-STK laser engraver.

All STK equipment is controlled by Compaq 386 computers using 16 MHz frequency and 200 Mbytes optical discs (stand 1990). The unique advantages of the Stork-STK MCD system are:

- extremely simple production of colour separations;
- time saving of approximately 30% to 40%;
- reduction in labour cost;
- tremendous savings in production materials;
- improved quality and different resolutions on the X and Y axes are possible;
- extremely accurate fitting of the design;

- facilitates the quick realisation of new ideas;
- increases competitiveness;
- uncomplicated operation – thanks to simple menu technique anyone with a minimum of colour separation knowledge can successfully operate this equipment;
- very short training time;
- the Stork-STK MCD system is compatible with large mainframe CAD systems like Scitex and Siemens-Hell, as well as to the Stork X-cel ink jet printer.

The Tiba way of using CAD

The preceding paragraphs show that our company is currently using three types of CAD/CAM equipment. While these come from various manufacturers and were not bought at the same time, all are fully compatible. The compatibility of the newly acquired or modernised equipment with that already in use had constantly been on our mind. When upgrading the Response 220 type to the Response 280 version we also bought a two-way interface for the Stork-STK system. The equipment is thus capable of producing input data for the Stork-STK system but it can also process the data produced by it. This makes it possible, for example, to use the input from the TS 87 Stork-STK b/w scanner for the Response system and then to carry out the film's exposure by an ELP (electronic laser plotter). It is also possible to use separation recordings from the Stork-STK systems for this purpose. Our Stork-STK system is further equipped with a Kennedy Universal tape reader which can read magnetic tapes in the Scitex format and produce from them input data for the system. This equipment was valuable for us when we were using the old Response 220 system without a two-way interface.

The Desitex V CAD system produces recordings in the Stork-STK format and this makes it fully compatible with the Response 280 equipment. This versatility of our CAD systems is of great practical importance to our company.

As mentioned before, three groups of printing machines are used by the Tiba printing workshops:

- flat film printing machines;
- cylinder film printing machines;
- cylinder printing machines (photogravure).

While the processing of designs for cylinder printing and cylinder film printing with a galvanic screen can be carried out by any of our systems, only the Response 280 equipment can handle designs with a hazure or a hexagon. This means that we do not have to think hard where and how to process a particular design, because in the final stage we can transfer it on to the Response 280 equipment, making both the hazure and hexagon available. We are also able to tackle the frequent changes in the required printing technique; the mutual compatibility of our equipment enables us to solve such situations without much trouble. The designs are distributed for processing to the CAD equipment which is best suited to handle the given type of design (Fig. 8.4).

Further perspectives of using the CAD systems

The present abundance and variety of CAD systems competing on the world market makes it difficult for the potential user to choose the one best suited to his needs. That does not stop the design studios as well as textile manufacturers, large and small, from applying them in ever increasing numbers. These systems have their use in all areas of textile manufacturing, be it the creation of designs, the measuring of colour values or the creation of cuts for ready-made clothing. There are systems that form a part of jacquard and knitting machines, as well as those designed for special purposes such as the CAD system of CGS for the control of printing used with the Chromojet printing unit and the like. An unbiased evaluation of individual systems'

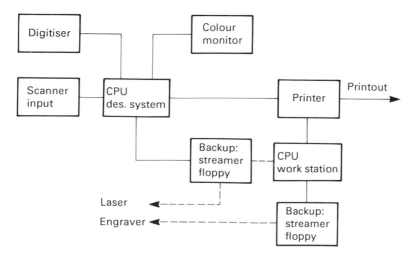

Fig. 8.4. Configuration of CAD/CAM systems in Tiba.

advantages is possible only after long-term practical use. There are surely other systems that could successfully be put into operation by our company, such as the CAD type 100p by High-Tex or the Create Design EX of the Benz corporation; also the systems of HCS Computer Graphics 'IGOS', the CIM (computer-integrated-manufacturing) made by CIM Textil Ltd, the CIM system supplied by CAIPO Engineering System, the colour composer of Van Dietmar Electronics, the Tex Sim, Tex Style and Checkmaker design system by Mitsubishi, the CAD/CAM system of IAM, the CDI 2DPC system by Computer Design Inc., the Mikado textile design system of Cositex, the Design 3 system by CIS Graphik, system Pastec 3000 MX by Dainippon Screen, or the equipment supplied by Crossfield, to name but some.

The application of further systems by Tiba will depend on their use. At the moment we shall certainly concentrate on increasing the creative and processing capacity for the textile print designs because their numbers increase year by year while the number of metres going to each design in production is steadily decreasing. This is caused by the situation on the market which requires short runs of the individual designs and their frequent changes. The number of designs we process has risen by 35% since 1985. The 'quick response' requirements make us search for the best ways to fulfil orders in the shortest possible time and thus put ourselves in a better position in the market.

We are considering the application of the so-called MCD (manual computer design) systems manufactured by Stork-STK, which would greatly speed up the preparation of designs now processed by hand only and for which the use of CAD systems would be uneconomic as a necessity. We are further contemplating CAD systems for creative purposes, but there also seems to be an urgent need for a large format colour scanner. Until now the scanners most widely used with CAD systems (Sharp, Howtec) could scan artwork in up to A3 (DIN) format only; for larger designs this procedure has to be repeated several times. As for outputs we expect to introduce a Stork X-cel jet printer for specimen printing on the kind of fabric to be used for the final product. It would enable us to see in advance what the respective design would really look like. We also intend to link our CAD systems to a colour measuring unit (a Datacolor or ICS).

As could be expected, the application of CAD systems within our company met with initial distrust among the employees. They looked at this equipment as if it were a mere computer and not a formidable means of making their work easier and faster.

Our experience proves that CAD equipment does not require staff with any special computer-oriented knowledge because today's CAD systems are designed for easy handling. On the other hand the CAD crew must know their ABC of textile manufacturing (artwork, repeating etc.). The greatest trouble we experience with our CAD systems is the 'language'; correct understanding of the orders and information given by the system is often more difficult than working it. Unfortunately not all our employees have a good enough knowledge of English or German. Even this problem can, of course, be solved. All it requires is time and money.

THE EDUCATORS

Chapter 9
Training and Education

JOHN HARVEY VALLENDER

John Harvey Vallender entered the bespoke clothing industry in 1967 and worked for fifteen years in a high class bespoke manufacturing retail organisation, specialising in pattern cutting. He entered the teaching profession in 1981; his specialism is pattern cutting and cutting room practice. He has cultivated an interest in information technology and computer aided design and machine management. He has become expert in the use of the Lectra CAD system in pattern development, grading and lay planning.

His industrial and professional qualifications include a full advanced certification in clothing technology, a Cert. Ed. and B.Ed. He has a particular interest in curriculum development and assessment. An accredited CBT (Computer Based Training) author and a member of the CFCI course review panel, he is committed to the fostering of industrial links with colleges. He is presently a lecturer at Handsworth College where he is also responsible for the provision of consultancy and bureau facilities.

Introduction

This chapter is intended for individuals who are developing learning materials for others, or for learners planning their own learning programmes in applied CAD. Its purpose is to share a number of ideas which may aid the process of learning to use CAD.

The chapter begins with a personal view of the nature of CAD systems, then considers some fundamental learning theories and attempts to link these to a possible learning process which may be employed for CAD. The chapter concludes by offering a simple description of a tested format for a CAD learning resource.

Let me start by making a general observation: 'learning is likely to be more successful if a learner appreciates the way in which CAD systems function'. This is not to say that a learner should have detailed technical knowledge of a system, but rather that they should possess a general overview of functions and limitations. When the learner knows what the functions are and is familiar with what can be achieved with a system, he or she is likely to be more efficient and effective when learning its use. (By system I mean an integrated set of component pieces of equipment and computer programs which have been collected together for a particular purpose.)

In other words, I am suggesting that successful learning is fostered if the learner approaches the task with a realistic conception of what can be done with a system and what to expect of it.

Computer systems have operational hierarchies and procedure, as do the software applications which are to run on them. These hierarchies are determined by the designers of the hardware and software. As a general rule, users of CAD systems do not have the authority or technical skills to change these hierarchies. Therefore potential learners are obliged to adopt, without amendment, the fundamental hierarchies, procedures and functions provided for them.

Put another way, a user has access to a hardware and software 'box of tools'. The tools included are arbitrary, any choice being associated with decisions on which tool to use. Users have to recognise and learn the primary function of each 'tool' and the correct way to use it. Failure to use a tool correctly will usually result in the system displaying an error message, and may in some cases cause the system to stop working ('crash'). Learning to use the tools is more to do with knowing that something operates and produces results rather than knowing how or why the tool is as it is. Only after learning the effect of pressing this key or that button in a certain sequence can a user begin to use a system for solving problems. Such learning must be accomplished before a user can exploit the latent potential of a system.

The powerful and exciting 'what happens if' nature of CAD is founded on a good vocational understanding of the problem to be solved, linked to and enhanced by appropriate use of the tools provided by the system.

The case so far is: the individual elements ('tools') available within a system are the property of the CAD system designers. The function of each tool must be learned without question, and once this has been achieved control moves from the designer of the system to the user. This occurs as the user begins to employ the tools in the system's toolbox in unique combinations.

A learning programme

This is an outline of a programme which the reader may consider adopting and modifying as a model for planning their own, or someone else's, learning of a CAD system. To assist a learner, a training manager must strictly and clearly determine initiation to a system. A manager must decide what is important for the learner to know, in what order this 'knowing' is to be acquired and how best to achieve it; in other words what curriculum needs to be planned.

To help in this, a training needs analysis should be considered. This should help to determine which of the tools in the CAD box the user needs to employ, and which are to be introduced and learned about first. It is a mistake to attempt to introduce the whole spectrum of tools in one programme. One of the most important features of training success in CAD and computing in general is for the learning process to provide success within realistic and relevant experience. A manager must protect a learner from being 'overdosed' and over-whelmed by 'the possible', and direct learning towards 'the appropriate'.

In an industrial environment the training need will be determined by a specific job/task description and will be directly related to a specific production process. In an educational environment the manager will need to select an appropriate production process or design problem to be solved, and this will form the basis for the job/task description.

The first step will be to learn about the selected tools to be used. The next step will be to provide examples and safe experiences which exercise and guide the learner in the application of these tools. The final step will be setting the learners free when they are confident enough to begin planning combinations and applications for themselves.

Thus the anticipated learning will at first be teacher centred, but as the programme progresses, the teacher's role will change to one of guide and then of resource. Conversely, the learner's role will at first be disciplined by the coherence of a strict subject matter, but gradually the learner will be expected to accept more responsibility for his or her own learning.

To achieve implementation of this programme, some thought must be given to how best to promote learning, and this in turn leads to some consideration of learning theories.

Learning theories

Learning theories can be polarised: at one extreme there are 'behaviourist or connectionist' theorists, and at the other extreme 'cognitive or field cognition' theorists. The fundamental difference between the two stems from their perception of the nature of the learning processes that humans employ.

The behaviourist views learning as a process of links between a stimulus and the response generated by that stimulus. Learning is seen as some sort of reaction and is expressed as a series of inputs and outputs, i.e. if this stimulus is done then that response will follow. Learners can be encouraged and motivated to 'react' to a specific stimulus in an expected manner. Thus it can be said that learning has taken place when a predetermined stimulus is followed by the required response.

On the other hand, cognitive theorists place the learner at the centre of the learning process and see learning as being proactive – a process based on internal thinking and the ability to be aware of the context and surroundings of an event in such a way that responses are flexible and valid but not necessarily reliable.

A crude comparison of the two perceptions can be expressed as:

- Behavioural learning is *externally* influenced and is done *to* the learner.
- Cognitive learning is *internally* influenced and done *by* the learner.

The behaviourist view

Behaviourist theorists such as J.B. Watson (1878–1958) and E.L. Thorndike (1874–1949) propose that undirected learning is accomplished when a random response to a stimulus proves successful, and responses are reinforced and established as learned when a given response to a stimulus repeats its success. Thus unsuccessful responses will be abandoned whereas repeating successful responses produces the appropriate stimulus response (S-R) pattern.

The theory goes on to claim that the more often a successful S-R pattern is exercised, the stronger will be the likelihood that a specific stimulus will generate its partner response; and further, that the sooner a response is seen to be a satisfactory conclusion of an initiating stimulus, the more likely the response is to be linked to that stimulus.

Perhaps the most influential behavioural theorist is B.F. Skinner, who proposed several valuable conclusions for training managers to consider:

(1) Each step in the learning process should be short and should grow out of previously learned behaviour.
(2) In the early stages learning should be regularly rewarded, and at all stages should be carefully controlled by a schedule of continuous and/or intermittent reinforcement.
(3) Reward should follow quickly when a correct response appears.
(4) The learner should be given an opportunity to discover stimulus discriminations for the most likely path to success (D. Child 1981).

Skinner suggests a distinction from the reactive learning expressed by Watson and Thorndike; he prefers to view the S-R partnership as being generated by the learner as he operates on his environment. Where Skinner's theories prove less useful is in illuminating what is going on inside the learner during the learning process. His work is essentially to do with the observable, external manifestations of learning. Skinner's conclusions about learning could well suit instructional type objectives, such as listing, stating, repeating and, for our purposes, some of the key pressing activities required of CAD.

Cognitive views

What seems to be missing are answers to some questions about meaning. What does learning mean to the individual? Surely there is more to human learning than can be explained by arrangements of S-R links. How is it that learners respond in different ways to the same stimulus? Cognition theorists argue that learners interact with a stimulus and that the response given is influenced by the learner's perception of an event, such learning is much more than a programmable response. The interaction is based on past experience and an understanding of the problem to be solved.

Founder members of the cognitivists movement were Köhler and Koffka; their particular school of psychology is known as 'gestalt' psychology. Perhaps their single most important contribution was their description of 'insight' as part of the process of learning, proposing that learning occurs when a solution to a problem is identified. That is to say a response to a stimulus occurs suddenly as the learner perceives the whole problem and is able to reorganise the elements of the problem by restructuring his fields of perception in order to determine a probable solution.

The emphasis in gestalt psychology is adaptability; learning is formed from and based on existing knowledge and experience, which is modified to accommodate new perceptions and understanding. In this way learners progress from a low level to higher levels in a continuous spiral of increasing understanding and knowledge.

The learning process

Although not fully explored, it should be apparent that no one theory provides all the answers to the process of learning. In practice the most justifiable approach seems to be to use that which appears to be appropriate in any given situation.

A summary of the theories suggests that learning does take place when a response satisfies a stimulus, and that events which occur close together and are repeated tend to be learned more permanently. Also, learning occurs when a problem is seen as a whole and the relationships between the parts and the whole are restructured in context, using the resident knowledge of the learner as a base for progress and accommodation.

Put another way, it seems that successful learning can be achieved without recourse to understanding, but equally that learning can also be achieved through logical analysis which is dependent on understanding.

If this is true, is it useful to distinguish between these two apparent types of learning? If designers of curricula can recognise specific value and application in both types of learning – learning without understanding and learning based on understanding – then it follows that a curriculum should employ, encourage and exercise appropriate types of learning as required.

Take for example the initiation phase mentioned earlier. Learners may need to connect the various parts of the system and what happens when they press certain keys (in other words build S-R links). Later they will need to link series of key strokes as a procedure.

Questions to be answered at this early development stage are: Do the learners need to know why a key press generates a specific response? Or do they need to know which keys to press to achieve a required response? I would suggest that initially it is the latter. Therefore a manager may need to develop a learning resource which is initially designed to facilitate a strong behavioural S-R approach, in order to establish a 'habit' of key strokes.

However, once initiation has been achieved and the knowledge it represents has been established, the learning resource can move on to proposing and testing hypotheses based on problems and the tools currently available. The learning resource will therefore begin by employing S-R tactics and will quickly move towards employing learning strategies which rely on understanding and meaning. The first part of the resource will seek to provide models of S-R relationships and give opportunities for learners to practice these relationships, the learning being supported by clear product oriented assessment, which to a large extent can be self-assessment. In other words, learners will be told what happens when certain keys are pressed, stimulated to press these keys and rewarded for their success. Failure to secure the required response will initiate a remedial loop which will be followed with limited variation until the required S-R pattern is established.

The remainder of the resource will seek to establish cognitive learning associated with creative, analytical and evaluative thought. Having learned by rote that this or that key produces a specific response, the learners have to begin to plan how to link key presses in order to achieve specific ends. They have to begin to develop and use cognitive maps in order to construct efficient and effective strategies, otherwise their learning is unlikely to progress past the lowest level of trial and error.

The Piaget model of learning

Jean Piaget, a Swiss psychologist (1896–1980) proposed a model of learning which seems to be particularly useful for designers of curricula where cognitive processes dominate. Piaget's model was developed from a study of the development of childhood intellect, but the insight it gives to this branch of cognition is no less valuable in the development of CAD knowledge for adults.

Piaget proposes that 'real thinking is logical and follows the rules of logic'. Thus the goal of learning to use CAD is seen as a move from a situation where the environment, the computer's own hierarchy in this case, is overwhelmingly in control, to a situation where thought processes respond to the logic of the situation and judgements are based on the logical relationships between the CAD system and the problem to be solved.

The first stage towards developing this control begins with the successful interpretation of symbols: a system symbol becomes 'owned' by the learner in that the symbol holds personal meaning for the learner. Piaget suggests that such ownership is facilitated by the mode of imitation. Thus practice is vital to the successful construction of the logical learning sets that a learner uses to deal with a situation. (Piaget calls these systematic and co-ordinated learning sets 'schema'). Piaget put forward the proposal that learners change their current learning sets in order to accommodate new knowledge, and that if the new knowledge is too far removed from their 'base' schema, learning is unlikely to occur. (A learner will try to know and understand a new situation by comparing it with what is already known and understood).

Any changes to the schema are assimilated by the learner during inventive and imitative practice. Once accommodated and assimilated, revised schema can be used in similar situations of logic in the future. A learner literally builds his own knowledge by this accommodation and assimilation process. The implication for designers of learning materials must be that a careful progression of experiences should be provided which take the learner from where he is to a higher level of understanding and knowledge.

With understanding it is possible for a learner to recognise how a sequence of events lead to a conclusion, so when the learner is presented with a similar problem he can use his knowledge to think back from the current problem and propose solutions based on a previously tested schema. Thus design analysis and strategic planning are more firmly based on the probable than the possible.

The implication of this model is that learners should be challenged with problems that contain familiar elements, but that the elements should be presented in novel ways. In terms of designing a learning resource intended to develop knowledge, Piaget and fellow cognitivists' ideas can be expressed as: A learning resource should help the learner to:

(1) become aware of a problem;
(2) clarify the problem;
(3) propose hypotheses for the solution of the problem;
(4) reason out the implications of the hypotheses;
(5) test the problem against experience.

Put another way, development of knowledge is about interacting with the problems of the environment by applying to each problem a scientific and logical method of intelligent enquiry. Specifically for CAD the learning resource should be designed to:

(1) initiate the learner into the rules of a CAD system;
(2) demonstrate and provide practice in fundamental CAD procedures;
(3) demonstrate and provide practice in design analysis;
(4) demonstrate and encourage logical planning in the use of CAD simulation;
(5) encourage experimentation based on planning execution and evaluation of CAD simulations for vocational problems.

Model for learning CAD

It should be clear by now that I subscribe to the view that, for the most part, learning is something that the learner has to do. Therefore a learning resource should be designed to help the learner learn, rather than to teach to the learner – a resource which is capable of establishing specific and general rules in an efficient and informative fashion, but flexible enough to allow for knowledge to be understood in an efficient but personally relevant and meaningful way.

In other words the mode will be essentially 'learner centred', by which I mean much more than the learner working at his own pace and being able to pick and choose entry points based on his prior experience. Learner centred in this case means a resource written with the learner first and the content second. The resource is expected to:

- provide initiation to predetermined procedures;
- provide opportunities for practice and reflection;
- provide opportunities for negotiating exercise material which is relevant to the learner;
- encourage logical planning;
- be flexible enough to allow learners with different and or low/high levels of experience to plan their own learning strategy.

Such a resource may be expected to open with a brief description of the CAD application to be used and the CAD system itself, and then transfer quickly into the initiation phase. The amount of new information at each stage will be kept to a minimum and each piece of information or practice builds on the previous one(s). In the early stages the learner will be given a description of what to expect and will be invited to imitate the activity being discussed (i.e. establishing S-R partnerships). Later the learner will be presented with a more complex series of procedures and will again be invited to imitate using prepared sequences in the form of algorithms. Finally, the learner will be given a number of design problems to solve (i.e. establishing new schema by accommodation and assimilation).

Assessment of learning at this stage can be based on self and/or peer group. At the end of each stage a summary of activities should be given and at the end of the work an appendix of procedures may need to be provided as a quick reference. Consider using the first person, and keep computer jargon reduced to the essential. Too much jargon could exclude some learners. Wherever possible, assessment should be based on real and negotiated problems intended to facilitate and demonstrate that assimilation of CAD concepts and CAD practice has taken place.

Conclusion

This chapter has attempted to outline and justify a design process of a learning resource for CAD. It has looked at learning theory and recommended that a pragmatic approach should be adopted, where learning is seen as an activity of the learner accommodating and assimilating knowledge in a meaningful way. The 'teacher' is seen as a helper in this process.

It is important to re-state that the central function of the learning resource is to develop CAD thinking. As Jerome Bruner (1960), quoted by Dennis Child, put it: 'methods of inquiry are more durable than facts and even generalisations'. It is the students who have to learn, and they will do so best by interacting with their environment. Therefore to be helpful the resource will have to 'arrange' events in such a way that learners are encouraged to interact productively with, in this case, the CAD system being used. David Ausubel (1969), also quoted by Dennis Child, uses the term 'advanced organisers' to describe this activity.

To summarise, learning is something that learners have to do for themselves. In the first instance they have to learn what tools are available and what each tool does. They then have to discover, in a purposeful and directed way, how to use CAD – to develop an enquiring attitude towards the use of CAD in simulated solutions to vocationally oriented design problems.

Such discovery learning tends to imply learning based on the individual or on small group activity. Therefore the learning resource should in its latter stages permit individualistic learning without absolutely requiring it. Because, for most learners, CAD will be a new experience, the resource or package as it will now be called will need to facilitate a progression from teacher centred subject initiation thought to student centred hypothesising and evaluation. To execute this change the package must enable learners to shape and use the ideas being developed, in such a way that the learner contributes, applies, tests and evaluates the activities promoted by the package. In other words, it is essential that the learner constructs his or her own meaningful interaction using his/her own store of experience as the basis for extending knowledge and understanding. In practice this means allowing the learner to provide his/her own focus for learning and assessment problems.

A basic introduction to the learning theories discussed in this chapter can be found in the book by Denis Child, noted in the reading list below.

Suggested Reading List

Anderson D.C. (1981)   Evaluating Curriculum Proposals.
                              Croom Helm, London.

British Gas (1986)   A systems approach to training.
                              Futuremedia Ltd, Bognor Regis.

Child D. (1981)   Psychology and the Teacher.
                              Holt, Rinehart & Winston Ltd,
                              Eastbourne.

Further Education Unit   Curriculum Change – an evaluation of
(1981)   TEC programme development in
                              colleges.
                              Department of Education & Science,
                              Stanmore.

Further Education Unit   The Key Technologies – some
(1988)   implications for education and training.
                              Department of Education & Science,
                              Stanmore.

Further Education Unit   The Concept of Key Technologies.
(1989)   Department of Education & Science,
                              Stanmore.

Lee, D. (1975)   The Doris Lee Lectures – Curriculum.
                              University of London Institute of
                              Education, London.

Heathcote G. et al. (1980)   Integration or co-ordination.
                              NATFHE Journal, Feb 1980.

McNally D.W. (1977)   Piaget, Education and Teaching.
                              The Harvester Press Ltd, Hassocks.

O'Hear A. (1981)   Education Society and Human Nature.
                              Routledge & Kegan Paul, London.

Peters R.S. (1971)   Ethics and Education.
                              Allen Unwin, London.

Rowntree D. (1974)   Educational technology in curriculum
                              development.
                              Harper Row, London.

Sockett H. (1976)   Designing the curriculum.
                           Open Books, London.

Warwick D. (1987)   The Modular Curiculum.
                           Basil Blackwell Ltd, Oxford.

Chapter 10
Training and Education in CAD Clothing/Textiles Systems

JANE DEVANE

Jane Devane graduated from Cheltenham School of Art & Design with a First Class Honours Degree in Fine Art and gained a Masters Degree at the Royal College of Art, London. She received a Fellowship from North West Arts and was the Artist in Residence at Crewe and Alsager College of higher education. Jane Devane is currently a lecturer in Fashion at Cheltenham and Gloucester College of Higher Education, and is also textile tutor for the Open College of the Arts.

Introduction

As a practising artist and current course leader on a National Diploma course in fashion at Cheltenham and Gloucester College of Higher Education, I have welcomed the increased opportunity to explore the use of CAD in education. I am mainly concerned with textile design, fashion illustration and visual studies which combine basic design, drawing and colour. All these subjects are concerned with image making and so the introduction of computer graphics has had a strong impact on design education. It has generated the need for artists and designers like myself to understand, adapt and support the integration of various computer systems into the educational programme, and I feel strongly that good design courses need to take full advantage of this new form of visual communication.

For the last two years most of the students who have applied for a place on the Fashion Diploma Course have come equipped with basic computer experience. They may have started with an Amstrad at home for word processing and then at school have been encouraged to look at the creative ways in which computers·are used in the classroom. I have found that these novice fashion students already begin to think in different ways; they appear to rely more on each other and themselves to gain information and seem less dependent on the traditional tutor/student role. They are self motivated and anxious to take on board the technological advances being made within the fashion industry. Their enthusiasm to experience and research with CAD regarding fashion and textiles is amazing. They possess a very positive attitude to the present systems incorporated into our educational programme and within a short time can handle the most sophisticated equipment with great dexterity.

I am also a tutor for the Higher National Diploma course in Fashion Design Technology at the same college. As the course title suggests, it is a course of study for creative people with a preference for practical skills and a strong interest in fashion technology. The course was planned as a direct reply to the current needs of the fashion industry. As this is the first of a new and still rare kind of course – bridging the gap between creative design and fashion design technology – the use of computers in the different areas of the fashion industry forms the backbone of this course. Computers are its speciality and all students gain a reasonable degree of computer literacy during their two years of study.

Both Diploma and Higher National Diploma courses encourage students to use the well-equipped computer workshops to study colour, fashion graphics and textile design. The CAD projects set vary enormously from straightforward colour exercises and experimentation to work with video images for illustration and even to the construction of a three-dimensional object made from actual computer printouts.

There is also a cluster of terminals for general information technology, programming, graphics and for grading, lay planning and pattern cutting. We see our students employed as pattern cutter/ designers, computer operators/demonstrators in design rooms and computer companies, or as graders, lay-planners and designer/illustrators using CAD, and as designer/technologists for computer software companies requiring fashion expertise.

As new roles are created within the industry because of the increased use of computers for diverse functions, the potential employment market is growing rapidly world-wide. Final year students have found it easy to gain employment because the necessary computer experience was built into their work at college. One student recently produced an optical database with an historical context for designers and fashion forecasters, to enable them to make effective and useful design research. She worked in collaboration with Moda CAD and other CAD/CAM companies to assess current computer aided design systems. This same student will receive a research bursary to study and specialise in this area in greater depth.

Students studying the HND course can specialise in one aspect of the course during their last year. They can either work with an individual sponsor or gain additional work experience. Several students decided to specialise within the area of CAD and chose to explore pattern grading. With consultation from industry they compared the traditional methods and the advances being made with the impact of computer technology. Various computer systems were compared. Another student compared the traditional system and the Ormus PDS system both in pattern cutting and grading methods. Both students have gained subsequent employment within the fashion industry.

Integration in education

The recently changing attitudes of designers and artists towards CAD, and in particular its contribution to art and fashion education, have given birth to a new visual language whose creative, innovative and stimulating work can no longer be ignored. A new breed of fashion/ textile student is beginning to emerge. CAD/CAM is no longer a vision; it is reality in the fashion industry and therefore there have been changes and efforts made to incorporate the introduction of this technology and its far reaching implications into education. I am now optimistic about this integration having seen the results and the potential, but to begin with I had several reservations.

I like many others from a traditional Fine Art background, anticipated the technological advances in design education. However, I saw them independently and definitely outside the studio environment. Unfamiliarity with computer systems, the jargon and the medium led to an ignorance and distrust of their use – whatever that was. I did not wish to question or explore the seemingly complex functions of this sophisticated equipment which was always then housed in a sterile office environment. My reaction was to protest against any 'hands on' experience regarding my own work and I hesitated to employ any computer system when teaching or introducing drawing and textile projects to my fashion students. Nevertheless, as new systems were operated by these students with great success, I became aware of good things beginning to emerge. There were definite improvements in their presentation and illustration. The work they produced reflected an obvious interest and enjoyment. Their designs were creative, expressive and varied; problematic drawing skills had been overcome. If the students had given their approval for using computers in all subject areas, then it was time to find out why.

My initial approach to so-called 'economically efficient' work stations proved to be less daunting than I had first imagined. During a short period of staff development I started coming to terms with a Zenith, Paint Box and Cameo Paint. I was encouraged to ignore the lengthy and explicit manuals, ease of use being a priority. Words like pixel, menus, palettes, stylus or mouse were absorbed and then forgotten. Clever and creative designs evolved from a host of mistakes and wrong instructions.

With very little effort on my part the computer guided me through a considerable range of colours, effects and designs with a few clicks of the electronic pen. Within a short time I was able to experiment with various brush types, washes, pencils and chalk. Then it was on to flood filling, image merging and zoom functions, adding to the long list of impressive features. I came away thinking how easy it all was. I also became aware that having previously known nothing about computers and then sharing this learning experience with my students, a better working relationship resulted. Discussions on various software, the problems that face a computer-illiterate person, the embarrassments of drawing with a mouse and other relevant exchanges of information proved to be excellent therapy.

Differences in the medium

It was of course very different from holding a pencil on a piece of paper. I missed the feel of the texture of paper or canvas, the absorption of the paint or washes and the physical pleasure of creating an exciting surface or design with layers of chalk, wax, paint and collage. The spontaneous accident or mess found in the artist's studio, from which an interesting and original design might emerge, was impossible. I feel that surface texture and tactile materials are very important to a textile designer. Although it is now possible to texture map, taking a surface texture from a photograph and mapping it on to an image, this clever technique can only heighten realism on the screen, nothing more. Regarding drawing, students will always need to acquire the formal skills and sensitivity of practice from a drawing studio before they have access to the computer. The free-hand computer sketching ability can only reflect the students' own skills and general drawing ability.

One of the most frustrating limitations of any computer painting system is the actual size of work produced. I work on a large scale and therefore felt it necessary to manipulate small computer printouts using collage, repetition and other techniques. I have also encouraged students to think in terms of three dimensions on a large scale, whereby sculpture and weaving for instance with printouts can become an attractive and stimulating possibility. This manipulation and adaptation of CAD and its characteristics can be a fascinating area to explore. The results can be very interesting and can help to counter-

balance the disadvantages of this complex technology and break down the barriers that exist between the creative arts and the so called 'technology of science'.

Another problem is the screen. To sit for a long time in front of a screen that is only 10 in across its diagonal, fighting against the reflection of light, is not really conducive to producing good quality work. If you have 16 million colours it is vital to have a screen that can support them; no one wants a monochrome screen for CAD work.

It is useful to have a back-up of the screen in the memory, so that if you make a complete mess of something you can go back one step. If you have a good screen and a fast computer you do not want to use a keyboard to check designs. A mouse is not a suitable tool for good CAD; a graphic tablet and stylus is more appropriate.

Most of the computer art I have seen in recent exhibitions has shown some amazing images and ranges of visual effects. Whether or not this work has real artistic qualities is debatable. Artists who have decided to work with computers seem very intent on creating images that cannot be achieved by other means. They make use of the computer 'uniqueness'. Fantasy and reality often combine to produce exciting images. Pictures can be made with light instead of paint – the work of a computer scientist rather than an artist. It is all very advanced and reflects developments of image technology, but there is very little work where an artist has used the computer to produce drawn images that portray observations and an interest in subject matter around them.

When I decided to use the computer as a tool to create a new dimension to my own work, I realised that technical support is a must. Computers do amazing things but they need instructions and logical operations. Short introductory courses regarding their basic components and functions are a must. Although this basic theory can appear to be complex at first, one does not need a degree in mathematics to acquire the appropriate skills. Some students have said they would like to learn how to program a computer, so it will perform functions they might require of it. In my attempts to use CAD in my own work I soon realised how a computer can dictate, and that what one may have originally intended can suddenly change; you need little or no aesthetic sensibility to create a wide range of patterns and designs.

This is a problem, particularly in the training of students. They can easily let the computer interfere and impose its own structures on their images, which can make assessment and critical appraisal very difficult. In several projects I have found it hard to extract what the computer did and what the student intended it to do. The sheer quantity of work that can be produced by one student in a short time can also be a disadvantage as well as an advantage. The speed and the ability to accomplish a routine task such as experimentation of different colourways or to eradicate paint or mistakes very easily, do not have any relevance from a fine art stance but from a fashion or textile point of view perhaps they do. However, as a piece of equipment that can help create an image, store and manipulate it, the benefits for any creative person, fine artist or fashion student, are obvious.

CAD in fashion/textile courses

As the machines become more user friendly and easier to use, there is a need to concentrate on how students in fashion/textile design use them. The electronic systems work well as a creative medium in design education and they can portray what has been visualised imaginatively by any student, but students must be encouraged to adapt this technology to serve their own creative requirements.

The systems are not merely more complex but obviously very different from the conventional creative tools found in a stimulating college environment. It is now possible to combine photography, cinemotography, painting and drawing into one. But with this amazing box of tricks I find the students are usually loath to do any more to their computer creations. They see them as final statements or solutions that have been arrived at by complex exercises. However, in my projects I encourage them to photocopy, tear, enlarge, pleat, fold, work over these images using and incorporating other techniques, so that the progression of design development can continue and be seen as ongoing practice.

I feel very strongly that students should see CAD as an important accessory to other work. When I give a textile project to a group of students, the preparatory research, observations, drawings and experimental designs all exhibit very strong individual characteristics. When these are fed into the computer for further development, the results from the same group of students often appear to be very similar and repetitive. Obviously some students may have a preference for subtle colour while others prefer strong tonal contrasts. Most of the students will have taken advantage of repeat pattern, creating minor images and using 'cut and paste', but individual interpretation of ideas does seem lacking. It is only when this work is taken back to the studio for each student to reanalyse and refine his or her designs, that the work finally produced reflects individual intention and responses. Each student's creative ability can then be seen and assessed.

Most of the computer systems we have at college vary in price and performance but we do have a wide range of programs essential for CAD and computer graphics. Finding the space to accommodate this equipment and allowing access to large groups of students from many departments is a constant problem. We have recently adopted a booking system and a flexible timetable as a solution to the problem of demand and overcrowding. More importantly, we have full-time technical support, and the expert service they provide is invaluable.

Integrated projects, whereby fashion students can work in the photography and audio visual departments, are encouraged and the work they can create with the aid of computers allows these students to work frequently with high-technology media.

Choice of equipment

The question of which computers should be purchased for the training and education of CAD for fashion and textile students is not really necessary; the real question is 'What do I want to do and how can a computer help me do it?'. A computer expert and a designer want different things. How computers are used in industry may differ from how they are used in education, and the different needs and requests must be met separately.

As far as the computer industry is concerned speed is of the essence, but this is not a priority in education. Designers must use full colour even if they only have access to a nine pin dot matrix printer fitted with black ribbon cartridge. Designers are very rarely able to say what they want in terms of hardware. However, they do say that they would like to use a variety of brushes and drawing tools, to have a choice of colours from a large palette, to be able to erase easily, to block fill areas and draw smooth curves or generate squares and rectangles, and to make pure areas and create freehand shapes; the software range available for CAD is almost endless. It is important to have someone within the fashion department who knows what is required and can make sure the purchase of equipment will meet the demands of a fashion department and cater to the individual needs of a designer.

Our Lecturer in Design Computing has said that if he had a limitless budget, he would choose 'a system that comprised a computer with at least a 386 processor, 8 megabytes of RAM, a flat non reflective

20 in screen, an A3 graphic tablet and two buttoned stylus, a high speed hard disc drive with at least 120 Mbytes capacity, a 24 bit graphic card and video interface capability. As peripherals he would choose a Polaroid slide maker with PC interface and a sublimation printer of at least A3 capacity. His last comment was that he is always disappointed with the quality of printing.

With a restricted budget in education, providing the resources for CAD and its development will always be under constant negotiation and supervision. The introduction of CAD means fundamental changes in finance, perhaps with sponsorship from computer manufacturers likely in order that a progressive fashion course can keep up with the technological advances made.

Conclusion

I believe that to provide effectively the necessary computer technology required in a learning environment, information technology must enable fashion students to realise the applications, become familiar with the benefits and examine how they wish to use CAD as a medium. Our students are encouraged to question the use of computers and to evaluate when they should and should not be applied. They are made aware of this technology's potential and understand the advantages and disadvantages, but also realise that although each fashion course places a certain emphasis on the use of computers, it is not at the expense of traditional skills.

As a lecturer who works with a team, it is my role to nurture the understanding of colour, texture, shape and composition. The use of traditional drawing methods to strengthen visual awareness and encourage drawing for selection and visual information, play a key role in the development of each student's thinking within a fashion and textile context. The processes then help to build the visual vocabulary, and the exchange of opinions and ideas is the basic prerequisite of all artists and designers; the end product is an accumulation of all the processes and therefore not an end in itself. All this has been and can be achieved without the use of any computer system. However, there is no one way to develop the necessary skills and sensibilities required to create and design; therefore the introduction of CAD for experimentation and innovation can at the very least provide another alternative. As long as the focus of attention is on the quality of ideas and work, the aesthetic and design aspect of any fashion and textile course can be allowed to progress.

It is obvious the computers can contribute positively to design education. They are a medium through which personal creativity and originality can be enhanced and expressed. Their varied functions provide a platform from which to explore many exciting new areas that can stimulate and challenge an enquiring mind. Their speed is motivating because it allows a student to examine infinite alternatives before making a final design decision. In common with progressive elements in all areas of industrial development, this universal assistance of info-tech is an essential requirement.

However, the loss of some acquired skills though manual experience is bound to be a factor against sole computer design. This new technology must be seen as an instrument of assistance rather than a replacement technique. Imagination, initiative and intuitive response can be found and nurtured in any student but cannot as yet be found in any computer. The lack of interactive discussion between the user and the machine and the even greater lack of sensory facilities suggests that CAD has a long way to go yet. Only time and experience will indicate the limits to which CAD can be accepted.

Acknowledgements to Alan Villaweaver, Lecturer in Design Computing, for his advice.

VIEWS ACROSS
THE CAD FIELDS

Chapter 11
CAD for
Clothing and Textiles

GAVIN WADDELL

Gavin Waddell is a designer and an educator. He studied fashion design at St Martins School of Art in London. He was an assistant designer to two of London's 'Top Ten' couturiers. He was the designer and director of his own couture house, ready-to-wear dress company and fashion forecasting concern. He was a menswear designer to a Kings Road boutique in the 1960s and a freelance illustrator and designer for many British and international companies.

Gavin Waddell was Head of fashion and textile courses at Luton, North East London Polytechnic and Gloucestershire College of Art and Design. He is a member of the Fashion Board for the Council for National Academic Awards and Business Technician Council. He is a member of the Society of Chartered Designers and he is an examiner and assessor to many fashion courses throughout Britain.

He became interested in CAD while designing a new course for Gloscat. This interest led to a piece of published research for the Science Research Council. He is currently a visiting lecturer on design at Birmingham Polytechnic and Harrow College of the Polytechnic of Central London.

Introduction

My interest in CAD came about inadvertently, as a negative reaction to claims and assumptions I heard being made about my own subject – fashion design. Interested colleagues in other fields were applying their own attitudes and conclusions to my subject, and, I thought, clumsily applying these to a projected future of computer-led fashion design. I was so against these projections that I felt I must investigate the subject in a depth that satisfied my own professional conscience. I was, in fact, very sceptical at the outset, to the point where I questioned whether there was any future for CAD in the fashion industry at all.

I had been following the development of Computer Aided Manufacture and Computer Aided Technology (mistakenly so often referred to as Computer Aided Design) in the fashion industry for some time and had visited the very few companies that had installed computer aided lay planning, grading and in one or two cases computer aided cutting assemblies. The number of establishments that had any kind of computer technology could be counted on one hand.

Now under ten years later the number of computer aided units in the British fashion industry can be counted in thousands. I was particularly sceptical about the *quality* of design that could be achieved on the computer, having seen so many examples of the crude effects that had been perpetrated as 'design' in other fields, but was intrigued to find out what direct links were possible between CAD and the manufacturing process. As with much else I encountered at first, there was much talk but little hard knowledge except from those who were operating the systems 'on the ground'. Production managers and lay planners had taken over the role of directing the computer systems in the first factories I visited and they had become *very* knowledgeable indeed – knowledge acquired by trial and error, translating well-tried systems into a new language.

With a new race of technicians arising from this new technology, other roles in the fashion industry needed to be questioned and for my investigation the role of the fashion designer became crucial. Not only is the role of the designer put into dispute but the term design has very blurred edges, designers believing one thing, technicians another, the industry as a whole yet another and all further compounded by a general layman's view which has a rather romantic view of the whole activity. This would not matter to the designer were it not that any of these notions could affect the attitude and preconceptions of computer programmers planning new CAD systems for designers.

A research project in fashion design and CAD

This investigation later took the form of a piece of research for ACME – the Application of Computers to Manufacturing Engineering, a directorate of SERC, the Science Research Council – and was entitled Strategic Study to Investigate the Opportunities and Difficulties in Fashion Design for Automated Manufacture. My collaborators on this project were Paivi Makerini-Crofts and William Bates.

Initially we interviewed a sample of fashion designers, representing as we thought the many different facets of the industry from the design directors of multi-national companies and young designer-name companies, to design consultants and freelance designers. We looked again at the design process and what especially characterised fashion in this process. We reviewed the current fashion design CAD products. We wanted to know if there were aspects of computer automation which might de-skill a designer, and how the highly skilled designer could benefit from computer technology if there were plans afoot in softwear design houses for linking design into the existing computer aided pattern drafting, layplanning and grading systems. What design visualisation systems existed in other disciplines and could their techniques be applied to fashion? What future did the bureau design service have in design where small companies could buy time on expensive CAD/CAM systems. Could boring, repetitive time-consuming tasks be reduced, releasing the designer for creative design?

Designers on the whole were not sympathetic to the idea of computers, feeling that they could detract from, rather than enhance, the design process. They were worried about a loss of sensitivity and standardisation that the very character of a computer seemed to imply. Mechanical aids such as the stylus, VDU screen and plotter seem very far away from the soft lead pencil and the artist's drawing pad.

I concluded from interviews with designers and from the research generally, that the term design itself has its problems: the term has a completely different meaning to different people – designers, managers' technicians – in the fashion industry itself, let alone other areas of design. It is still under-rated and therefore defined in the lowest terms: 'stylist' or 'technician'. Its real innovative qualities are not understood even by practising designers, who quite often do not realise their real contribution to an industry that relies on their originality but is quite unprepared to acknowledge it. Technicians and production managers often see designers as a nuisance and the creative process as irrelevant.

I was also particularly struck by the fact that there appear to be two distinct *types* of designer, and not just in the fashion world. There is the designer who visualises the finished design in his head, is able to look at it from every angle, can make it walk up and down the catwalk, and sees the fabric, colour, cut details, buttons, trims, everything about it, accurately visualised and in a flash of a second. Then there is the designer who uses the sketch-book as a launch pad for new ideas; with this type of designer ideas come through drawing – very much in the manner of doodling – but carried to a much more sophisticated degree. This designer works from front and back views and therefore works in two dimensions. His translation to three dimensions takes place at the pattern cutting, toile making stage.

The former type of designer who visualises three dimensionally, in advance, uses drawing simply as a method of realising an already conceived idea. The latter type uses drawing to invent, visualise and develop ideas still unconceived. These two types operate at quite different speeds and require quite different help from any mechanical or automatic aids, so the most appropriate CAD specification for one would not necessarily suit the other.

On the whole the development of current sketching programs for the first type of designer is quite inappropriate. These draw what he would term a 'pretty picture' – in other words a weaker presentation of something he already sees much more clearly in his head. He needs a three dimensional modelling system to develop his already visualised idea. On the other hand the drawing designer could use adapted sketching systems to fit his design needs, but his drawing skills, sensitivity of line and personal techniques all help to invent his ideas and so far CAD sketching systems use conventional digitising tablets and stylus arrangements. Despite the latest innovations in more pressure sensitive pens, these systems lack the feeling of the 2B/HB/H pencil, rapidograph, brush, felt tip pen or even charcoal to help generate ideas on the pad.

It seemed to me that the second type of designer – the sketcher – was being catered for fairly adequately with the many sketching and paintbox systems on the market, but for the first type – the visualiser – and potentially the more interesting in terms of CAD development, very little had been done.

The nature of design and the CAD process

Because the real nature of design *is* either misunderstood or under-rated and because it was so difficult to get beyond the barrier of salesmen to the true designers of the CAD systems, I found it difficult to get a true picture of the present state of innovation in the field. Many people talked about 3D systems but either did not really know about them or were loath to divulge information to an interviewer who could leak new and highly profitable ideas or methods to com-petitors. On the other hand the more expert the person I talked to, the more tentative they were about the present state of development in this design field. Most said that a form of 'solid modelling' was near the answer, but that the drape/hang/movement qualities still needed to be developed – and this development demanded so many variables in the writing of the software that the time and money involved have put many companies off. Michael Starling at SDRC, one of the leading experts on solid modelling in the industrial/product design field, said in 1988 that it would take two or three years' hard work on the part of an expert team of software writers and designers to come up with a system that would satisfy both the fashion designer and the manufacturer. He did however believe that an 'engineer-led' industry such as fashion needed to develop a comprehensive CAD system to match its CAM developments.

The missing links in the chain from the design conception to final production of garments occur at the beginning and end of this chain. CAD/CAM itself can be a misleading term as it does not explicitly describe the middle section of the chain which, in fact, has been the most developed in the fashion industry: pattern development, grading, lay planning, costing and cutting. Some very important work has been achieved in specific design fields; Clark's 3D shoe design system is a good example. As far as manufacturing is concerned it is only the cutting, spreading and conveying systems which have been fully developed and are in current and common use, although there is a lot of work going on in the field of robotic garment production. Juki of Japan is one of the leaders, and fully automatic robotic garment manufacture must become a reality sometime soon. However it was the design end of the chain that concerned our research, and it seemed that nothing really had been done in fashion that could compare with the work that has been carried out in engineering/ industrial/product design where design systems can develop an idea in three dimensions from given specifications, can rotate, cover in a coloured skin, view from any angle in perspective and act as the model shop in the most sophisticated manner.

Graphics too have been similarly developed and are in everyday use, so familiar on our television screens. Architects and car designers were apparently using similarly sophisticated software. The difficulty with fashion is that it does not work in a rigid material like metal, plastic or concrete. Tweed, chiffon, taffeta, silk-jersey, acrylic and knit all move very differently and their hang and drape qualities entirely change the nature of a design. So far no real development has taken place in this area, presumably because the complex mathematical problems have yet to be overcome.

Types of design systems

Since the completion and publication of this research I have had the opportunity to look at an even more diverse range of computer aided design products, both here and abroad, and have tried to assess them in the light of our previous findings. There are three types of design systems currently available from software houses: the 2D design illustration/styling systems; the 2D illustration/styling systems that simulate 3D functions; and the actual 3D design systems. Most of the larger companies have integrated the first two, but only two houses – Computer Design Inc. in America and Modil in Belgium – have developed the latter, a truly 3D design system equivalent to the solid modelling packages available to product and engineering designers or Clark's 3D shoe design system.

Image creation

The 2D illustration system is most useful to the stylist designer who wants to sketch, visualise and produce attractive, saleable hard copy of his/her ideas in full colour with applied pattern and texture, much like a good colour photocopy. Most of the current systems have reached a level of sophistication that includes a huge colour palette, a fabric pattern and texture library, scanning and grabbing techniques and the possibility of scaling designs, patterns and textures up or down to a degree of accuracy that would never have been possible through manual draughtsmanship. For the commercial designer who needs to adapt and visualise, the possibilities are very encouraging. An image/figure design or diagram can be transferred to the screen either by drawing or tracing it on the digitising tablet or scanning it directly on to the screen from an existing drawing, illustration or magazine photograph. The 'brush' techniques are now so sensitive that the image can be drawn, coloured or adapted with a wide selection of 'brush' types that can simulate water colour, pastels, felt tip pen and broad or fine pen lines, can soften out hard edges and can erase unwanted areas. 'Brushes' can even pick up a texture either already in the menu or designed on screen; for example, a Prince of Wales or dog tooth check in selected colourways could be washed over a design, or an all over multi-coloured print could be applied to selected areas.

Sequential designing

Sequential designing – that is where a basic design is tried out with, for instance, alternative collar shapes, cuff shapes or pocket placing – can also be practised on screen, although the pixel systems I have seen cannot yet make diagramatic design quite accurate enough; the line always has an annoying wobble. The linear techniques used in most current pattern design systems are much more suitable for this kind of design and Ormus Fashion have developed a clever technique to overcome this problem. I understand, however, that the higher the resolution of screen and/or printer the less the wobble shows up.

3D design

As I mentioned previously, truly 3D design systems have only to my knowledge been developed by two companies, in the USA and Belgium. These are the fashion equivalent of solid modelling packages used by product and engineering designers, and can generate three dimensional images from two dimensional data. The wire framework so familiar in computer graphics is superceded at the American company by a 'framework' of dots which forms the basis of a sophisticated solid modelling technique. The 'framework' can take the form of a transparent tailored jacket or tailor's dummy, and style lines, panels, revers etc. can be plotted. The image can then be rotated and viewed from every angle. Using waist, hem and bust perimeters, a series of intermediate points can be generated including folds, bumps and curves. This 3D image can then be flattened into 2D diagram-pattern pieces.

The system I saw also included a skin function: the form can be covered in solid colour, print or weave – again all the visual effects we are used to seeing in computer graphics or solid modelling techniques, only with a fashion bias.

The problems regarding the hang and drape function (the algorithms needed to program these functions are, I understand, some of the most difficult to calculate) are not as it happens particular to fashion as the American company have worked with Chrysler on this problem to show the stretch and drape of car seat fabric, and are currently incorporating this function in their fashion design package. It appears that the hang could probably be given a specific gravity co-efficient which could, I presume, be matched with specific fabrics, say jersey, chiffon, taffeta, tweed etc. It should be added that I can find no British fashion company with sufficient confidence in 3D development to warrant their investing in a 3D system.

However, a 2D system can have all the essential function needed by the designer/pattern cutter; one such system, developed primarily as an educational tool for student designers by Ormus Fashion, allows the operator to match linear sketches on screen to a simultaneously drafted pattern alongside, developed either from adapted blocks already stored in the system or digitised from the designer's own blocks. A great advantage of this system is that it incorporates both linear and pixel modes. This means that diagramatic designs can be drawn in one mode and colour and pattern and texture can be applied in another obviating the disadvantages that these modes can have if used for the wrong purpose (as in the case of trying to draw diagramatically with a pixelated line, which looks so very shaky). This system had some very interesting pointers for the commercial world and has subsequently been developed commercially for the industry.

The designers use of CAD

Fashion designers must overcome their reluctance and learn to practise with all these new tools provided by the computer. They must try out as many systems as possible before they or their company is persuaded to invest in one or other of the fashion CAD packages or even dismiss them out of hand and also have in mind the future compatibility that any CAD system will have with computer aided pattern design, grading, lay planning, cutting head, manufacture and conveyor functions.

With the great advances in CAD being made in printed and woven textiles, fashion designers will have to get used to, and be able to assess, the possibilities of fabrics generated and viewed on screen with only hard copy colour 'photocopies' as sample swatches.

Now that comparatively small manufacturing units in the fashion industry are finding it worthwhile to invest in computer aided grading, lay planning and cutting equipment as the price lowers and the flexibility increases, so design or what is inelegantly called the 'front end of the industry', must take up its rightful place in the CAD/CAM design-manufacture-distribution sequence.

The computer should mean the dawning of a new age for the designer, for the many constraints that have held the designer back in the past *could* now be overcome. Theoretically a designer could be housed anywhere, could design individual items, ranges or collections on screen, cut the pattern automatically, grade, lay plan and pre-set a complicated manufacturing program, all from the desk top. This would mean that many of the agonies of pattern cutter-designer liaison and production and manufacturing hang-ups were obviated, although this is not quite yet the case so far, but it could be.

However, fashion designers have not taken to computers. They feel they spell mechanicalness, conformity, a loss of artistic licence, a sell-out to the technological age which they do not feel they are part of and which has never been sympathetic to the designer's ethos. Much of this problem or misunderstanding is that, on the whole, hardware and software companies have not really taken the trouble to understand how the designer works or what motivates him/her. Software designers have *imagined how they think designers think and work*, have based assumptions on superficialities, like the appearance of the designer's sketch, and have built a whole complicated and expensive system around this false premise. They have looked only at the styling element of design – often just a recolouring, refabricating rerun of a 'lifted' design – and then fed this back to the designer as the ideal design package. No wonder the best designers have been put off; not only has their art been entirely misunderstood and misrepresented but no one even bothered to consult them. Presumably, from past experience in other disciplines, calculating computer companies have found that if they can sell their product to thrusting managing directors whose designers just have to fall in line, inevitable modifications and alterations required by the designers will be fed back to the companies automatically; although from my own enquiries, surprisingly companies seem to have been somewhat lazy in this department.

This was particularly brought home to me in our own research for the Science Research Council. There were of course some notable exceptions, as in the case where the system had been designed by a designer. I also understand that even in the case of the really sophisticated industrial design solid modelling packages, industrial designers are reluctant to use their systems. There is always the danger that a kind of uniformity appears to be achieved – a restricting format. The screen, its size and shape, the quality of line and colour, the inbuilt *style* of computer graphics – all these elements can be frightening to the designer and his fragile talent. None of these considerations, however, have been addressed properly by either the designers or the computer companies, and certainly not as they should be – by the two jointly.

In an age where even government is more concerned with presentation than content, it is probably little wonder that this 'King's new clothes' syndrome has manifested itself in some design thinking and has had a confusing effect on those who have to plan strategies for designers. The confusion between illustration drawing and design drawing (where the embryo design idea is brought to life) is further confused in computers by the sophistication of computer graphics: a discipline based on illusion – representing items that do not and need never exist. Drawing for design, on the other hand, is about items that will have to exist and the medium of drawing is used, by the designer, expressly to test, explore and specify an idea in reality and eventually of course into manufacture. This is further complicated by the phenomenon of the two types of designer that I outlined earlier. In many ways the test, explore and specify qualities of properties drawing are eminently suitable to the capabilities of the computer and are one of the areas that really need to be exploited in fashion design.

Companies are of course improving their systems all the time and it is interesting to look at particular companies and their specialities. A British company, Cybrid, for instance, has developed a pen/stylus that is cordless and can function for left- or right-handed operators. Its sensitivity and variable point pressure give it more the feel of pencil or pen. Hand to eye coordination is thus much improved because the natural hand movements of a designer (describing an arc with a single wrist movement, flow of line, variation of thick and thin line) are the nearest so far to the sketch pad and pencil. One of the great drawbacks of the digitising tablet and stylus has been its lack of 'feel' for the designer, who can overcome this by scanning in a previously drafted sketch rather than draw freehand on the tablet or trace over an existing drawing.

This same company has also developed a diagrammatic linear mode which means that curves, angles and straight lines can be drawn with a satisfying geometric degree of accuracy; and items such as revers, jacket hem curves and yoke shapes can be very much more convincing. In the pixelated mode any drawing of this type looks very clumsy. Colour mixing has become much more sophisticated and many different methods, or even choice of methods, are being offered by most companies. Many designers will have to brush up on their colour theory to exploit the systems to the full. Printout colour grid pages of real subtlcty can be matched against paint, fabric or Pantone notation. Colours on screen can differ quite considerably from the chosen fabric sample, and although many companies are working to overcome this some operators can now do this adjustment in their head!

An American company who previously concentrated on CAD systems for knitwear now offer a full design system with a most interesting history of costume and history of art option (Moda Cad by Monarch Computex Corp). This means that a specific costume reference drawn from a large data bank, for example a 1959 Balenciaga dress, can be viewed on screen and used as direct design reference. Similarly the history of art package has references in the form of paintings, for example the Elizabeth I 'Ditchley' portrait by Marcus Gheeraerts, and in demonstration I was shown the embroidery from her skirt lifted to form the motif for a textile range.

The range of hard copy options is now quite impressive: an on-screen image can be photographed on a matrix camera, videoed on a print recorder, or using an extra high resolution thermal or ink jet printer a printed image of very high quality can be achieved. The thermal and ink jet printers have now largely superseded the others as they look most like a finished piece of designer's art work.

Current use of CAD in the fashion industry

It is interesting to see how the fashion industry is actually using CAD. Margaret Newlands, the Product and Design Director at Jaeger, tells me that CAD has become an integral part of the design process for their company. They use it to recolour prints to house or season's colours, for the design of prints and printed scarves, embroidered T-shirt motifs, knitwear patterns, and even for shop merchandising to make sure a season's colour/fashion story is maintained throughout all the stores in the country. They have delegated all the CAD work to a most skilful CAD Systems Adviser, Josephine Hole, who inteprets the design team's needs on to the computer and can thus produce very high quality printouts of print ideas, border prints, embroidery motifs and knitwear designs to each designer's specifications. Their printer is of very high quality and resolution and the fact that it produces matt printouts almost indistiguishable from a print designer's gouache means that the design team do not have to adjust to a new set of visuals. They, like most companies that are experimenting with CAD, have only so far invested in a 'paint box' system, albeit of the most sophisticated type, and have it seems no plans as yet to try any of the 3D design/pattern making systems even though these in theory could feed directly into their computer aided manufacture. Further development is still needed to convince these large fashion companies.

Conclusion

Despite all these exciting possibilities, designers and the companies producing CAD packages, either through fear or meanness, have not yet collaborated to their mutual advantage. CAD producers seem to be afraid of the experienced vocal designer, preferring to employ and be advised by inexperienced college leavers who will not 'rock the boat' or ask awkward design questions, and who presumably demand much smaller salaries. Designers, on the other hand, are wary of a new and untried medium and cannot risk either their own or their company's investment in a very expensive product whose advantages have yet to be proved. This is short sighted by both parties, for although the experienced designer would certainly want to ask awkward questions and change perceptions, he would, once won over, be the most convincing promotor.

Designers still reluctant to experiment are further put off by a sales pitch in which inexperienced demonstrators and extremely inept and inappropriate demonstration samples are the only means of judging the product's worth. Although student designers now have many opportunities to experiment on computers (most colleges have installed some type of CAD system) professional designers do not have this opportunity, and that time-worn phrase 'hands on' is still really the only method of understanding and judging the true potential that the computer can bring to design. More and more of our experienced designers should, somehow, be given the opportunity to experiment and discover for themselves the exciting potential of CAD.

Acknowledgements

To gather the material for this chapter I have had to survey, review or have demonstrated the following design systems:

Assyst-Assygraph, West Germany.
CDI Computer Design Inc., USA.
Cuttex, Switzerland.
Cybrid Fashion Designer, UK.
GGT. Gerber Garment Technology-Gerber Creative Designer, USA.
Ivestronica-Invesketch, Spain.
Lectra-Lectra Sketch 350+, France.
Microdynamics-MicroDesign, USA.
Modil, Belgium.
Monarch Computex Corp. Moda Cad, USA.
Ormus Fashion Education & Ormus Fashion Industrial, UK.

Chapter 12
Changing Attitudes

KAREN MACHIN

Karen Machin has a B.Sc. in Civil Engineering and gained an M.Phil. in Computer Aided Drafting at Hollings Faculty, Manchester Polytechnic. She has experience across a wide range of applications on CAD systems for the clothing and textile industries. She has also developed computer programs, as well as using systems in industry. She is now working in CAD at the Royal College of Art, London.

Introduction

Although many people in the clothing and textile industries have adopted computers, there are still many more who have totally misconceived ideas about this new technology. This is not limited to people who have worked in the industry for many years. There are still students leaving colleges who have either never used one, or who have had such little contact with them that they regard them as a complete mystery. This situation cannot continue: there is increasing pressure for companies to computerise their operations now that the existing systems are proven. For companies keen to invest in this equipment, two stumbling blocks are always quoted – cost and personnel. I would add a third – attitudes.

The cost of the systems is obvious on initial consideration of the equipment. The price of the subsequent maintenance contracts and supplies of durables, such as pens, paper and disks, also need to be considered. CAD systems do represent a large investment for any company, although the benefits can justify this initial and continuing cost. Personnel to use the equipment can be a problem because there is no existing pool of skilled people to operate these relatively new machines.

These two hurdles of cost and personnel are real problems for prospective purchasers, but they are difficulties faced when making any investment in equipment or staff. They are everyday problems for financial and personnel experts. The third problem of attitudes affects everyone and is far more wide-reaching – and it cannot be left to any expert.

What attitudes?

It is too simple to look at the marvellous examples of how computers are being used in the industry, to pat ourselves on the back and state that, with all these applications being used, every one of us is aware of them, understands them and has no prejudice against them. Any operator can provide annoying, specific examples of other people's attitudes towards computers. Take three examples: people still stand watching the plotter churn out another marker saying, 'Isn't it clever'; they still ask that irritating question, 'How will the computer grade this pattern?'; they still tell visitors fabricated stories of the remarkable feats the computer will perform. The operators' perceptions of other people's attitudes towards their machine are perhaps best shown by revealing that many joke, 'Blame it on the computer; everyone else does'.

People often assume that computers are used by technologists who, once they can use one, can use any. This may be true in some instances since it is certainly easier to use a second application after using a first. The knowledge of the operating system may be common to both; the hardware, such as the keyboard, screen and printer, may be similar. But, although this standard equipment may be used for a whole range of applications, it is usually purchased for a specific use. It will be placed on one person's desk or in a particular department. The application is far more important to its description than the fact that it is a computer. The skills of the operator are mainly those that they apply using it, not entirely those of using it.

In the clothing and textile industries, the term 'computers' could refer to any one of a range of applications from stock control systems to sewing machines. The expression 'CAD systems' is often used by computer-literate people to differentiate graphics applications from the rest. This phrase could refer to paintbox systems, pattern cutting, grading and lay planning systems or computerised looms, although there are obvious fundamental differences between these applications and between the skills of their operators. Each of these CAD systems is still referred to in practice as 'the computer' because the alternatives are too lengthy or obscure, and because it is often the only computer used by those specific people.

The very word 'computers' brings a range of reactions towards them from a general mistrust and fear to an unreasonable admiration. At one extreme there are people who hate them and regard them as an unnecessary evil. They often switch off at the very mention of the word. They consider them to be too difficult for normal people to use and only of interest to young 'whizz kids' who learned them at school. They feel that they are boring and logical, that they de-skill jobs and make the work repetitive and mindless. At the other extreme are people who think of a computer as some kind of magical machine which will transform the world overnight and by itself. They imagine a clean high-tech room where the operators, if they exist, punch a few keys and all the work comes out with no human effort.

Both these groups credit the computer with more power than it has. But where the technology haters will say that it cannot do the work as well as a person, the idolisers of it will be amazed that it can produce the work so painlessly. Neither group sees it for what it is – a useful tool. They have never used one and cannot comprehend why they should. They will continue to avoid them for as long as possible, preferably by employing someone else to use them.

Other people have specific complaints about computers based on a general awareness of them. These people have had a brief introduction to computers and have formed their own opinions, but this has hindered, rather than encouraged, them in further investigation of the systems. They repeat the obvious critiscisms and use these as excuses for not using them. If they continued using the existing equipment they would find that it can be tolerated. The current systems may not be ideal, but they are often preferable to returning to manual methods. Of course, some of their complaints are totally unrealistic. Without a thorough understanding developed through familiarity with the equipment, they cannot be expected to produce sensible criticisms all the time.

All these people prefer to leave the use of computers to the computer experts. They might complain that the systems do not reflect the requirements of the clothing and textile industries; they may say that it is obvious that the manufacturers have not consulted with the end users; but they themselves are not prepared to become involved. Eventually they will be forced to reconsider their attitude towards computers.

Whose attitudes?

The computer and its operators do not work in isolation. They have to work with people in other departments and representatives of other companies. These people may provide information for the operators or receive work from them. The results of their own work may directly affect or be affected by the computer. It is of fundamental importance that they all have a positive attitude towards this new technology. There will be difficulties in introducing a computer where people are unaware of how it will affect their work. If they are resentful of the new system they cannot be forced to use it successfully. If they think it will perform miracles they are likely to become disappointed with it. Their opinions about the system must be based on reality and not on rumours.

The senior management of the company must have an awareness of the potential uses of existing systems as well as an understanding of implications for the future. Five years ago there were many people who thought paintbox systems would never be applicable to the clothing industry. With advances in the development of suitable printers, these systems are now becoming more popular. The information that is held on these machines may have uses throughout the manufacturing process, just as data from the grading and lay planning systems can be useful for other departments. Full computer integrated manufacture (CIM) is a long term aim for the future. Senior management must have a knowledge of what information can be obtained from each system, who else could use it and how it can be transmitted.

Consideration of future plans must also include an awareness of the people entering the industry. There is an existing generation gap in attitudes towards the systems. Young people in their twenties have had access to computers at college or school. They may not have a detailed knowledge of them, but they are aware of them and prepared to use them. Many people of their parents' age, in their forties or fifties, have not had this access and are understandably apprehensive. The difference in attitudes over this twenty year age gap is considerable, but it is minor compared to the changes we will see in the future. Children of ten years old have a completely different view to people only ten years their senior. Computers are taken for granted in their world since they have always been there and affect everything – their schoolwork and toys, their music and films. They will expect to use them when they leave school. Older people need to develop this same attitude. They have already learned the manual skills applied using the computer and will have to share this knowledge with less experienced workers. They must learn how their traditional skills can be applied using these new tools.

There is another gap between attitudes of different people: the difference in perception between designers and their technicians. This is understandable as, for the last twenty years, computers have been used for the more technical applications. For example, in the fashion industry designers are unfamiliar with the grading and lay planning systems because they are not usually involved in performing these tasks manually. This in itself cannot continue if they wish to remain up-to-date in their production techniques. With the advent of affordable and more powerful paintbox systems, it becomes imperative that designers can use computers.

Everybody involved with the clothing and textile industries, at all levels, needs to be aware of the possibilities of using computers in their work. Eventually it will become impossible to avoid them as they will affect all parts of the production process.

Why do these attitudes still exist?

Over the last twenty years computers in general have become ever more sophisticated and powerful, with a corresponding decrease in their physical size. Machines which used to need a room of their own now occupy a desktop. They are no longer banished to a mysterious computer room, but are an everyday object to be found in most offices. Everyone has used one in some disguise and yet the previously described attitudes still exist.

This is perhaps because computer systems are at a certain stage in their development. Only ten years ago very few clothing manufacturers had grading and lay planning systems. Only the very large companies could justify the cost of this very expensive equipment, and smaller companies could not have anticipated that one day they too might be able to afford them. As the price has decreased, so more companies have become interested in their purchase. Paintbox systems have only recently become available in a form which can be used successfully. Although CAD systems have been around for many years, they are still relatively new and a very limited number of people have used them.

Historically, operators tended to be with a company at the purchase of a system. Training courses were provided for purchasers; there were no courses for people already in the industry to learn about the use of CAD unless they were going to use it for a specific company. This has led to a situation where computer operators are seen as some special kind of person. The vast majority of people do not have access to the systems, so those who do use them must be 'computer people'.

It could be argued that there is no point in learning about a CAD system until it has to be used. Until recently, each system was unique and the new user required a lot of practice before feeling confident with it. In order to use another application another complete training course had to be endured, followed by more practice. Each training course was very expensive and could not be justified unless the person was going to use the system. To some extent skills learned on one were of use when using another, but the language and techniques involved were completely different. This situation is changing as the manufacturers constantly make improvements to the systems so that they are easier to learn. It is now possible to suggest a whole series of basic computer skills which can be applied with small variations to a range of systems, and which provide an introduction to the way computers work. This general type of information should be available to all who come into contact with computers, even if they do not use them daily.

This information should be common knowledge to people already experienced in the industry, who are needed to provide direction both in the use and the potential uses of the systems. Instead they delay the day when they become involved with computers, leaving it to younger, more computer-literate people to use the systems and waiting for the ultimate, perfect version to be released before they investigate. This is wrong on both counts. Computer skills are not an essential requirement before using the systems; a thorough understanding of the manual skills to be applied is far more important. Although the currently available systems could be improved, they do provide useful tools for certain applications. Becoming involved with them now does provide a whole list of benefits. It also ensures that the systems are developed as required by the end users rather than as imagined by the computer industry.

A change in attitude – an example

Criticism about the paintbox systems has centred on the opinion that designers will never use them. Computers are assumed to be boring, logical machines which will inhibit designers' creative thinking. Designers have, so far, been able to avoid them because so few companies have bought the systems and many employ specialists to operate them.

The example of fashion students at the Royal College of Art (RCA) challenges these assumptions on who can use computers. Students at the college are all postgraduates, but many had never had access to a computer before the RCA. Several students have commented that there was a computer at their previous college, but it was always used by the science or graphics departments. Accessibility of the computer is very important to fashion students. If someone else is using the system they will invariably find another method of working which will be quicker than waiting for computer time.

Most students had had no encouragement to use one as a normal tool for their work. Tuition on the systems was seen as a separate course distinct from learning the specific skills of fashion design. Many have said that they wish they had used them earlier. They can see that computers can aid them in their work, but feel frustrated by learning the techniques at this late stage.

There are two CAD systems in the RCA fashion department: a paintbox system and a pattern cutting, grading and lay planning system. Both of these are used voluntarily by the majority of students in the department.

The pattern cutting, grading and lay planning system has been used for all its traditional benefits. A library of the block patterns has been stored on the computer so that the students can find any pattern quickly and reproduce it accurately. They no longer have to search through a rail of card patterns to find that the one they wanted is already being used or that one piece of that pattern has been misplaced. They can quickly plot out any block pattern in any size. They can grade their own patterns and produce more accurate fabric costings. They can alter the patterns to reduce the fabric usage. These are all standard uses which can be taken for granted by people familiar with these systems. It is unusual that designers rather than pattern technologists have used them, and used them voluntarily.

More unusual uses have occurred because the students are not limited by the normal demands of production and they have more time to investigate new methods of working. Many have used the facility for drawing patterns to any scale, a facility which is rarely used in industry. Trevor Harrison used it to develop his own block shapes from patterns produced by modelling on a quarter-scale stand. He digitised the quarter-scale calico pieces to plot out full scale pattern pieces. Caroline Harding and Carolyn Randolphi, knitwear students, produced distorted pattern shapes on graph paper to show the number of stitches and rows required for their garments. This could be done very quickly by calculating the different scales for the axes, whereas manually it had taken hours.

New uses of the system have been entirely due to the fact that the students have applied their traditional methods of working. They are not computer specialists looking towards future developments of the systems. They are interested in using the available technology as a tool for their own work, and, not being typical users, they are constantly finding new ways of using the equipment.

The paintbox system has been developed specifically for fashion designers, has all the functions the students require and is easy to use. These systems are relatively new to the fashion industry and arguments for their use are being developed. These have concentrated on the reduction in costs and increased design response which appeal to the company managers buying them, but which are irrelevant to design students. They use it for a far wider range of work than would be expected from a consideration of the manufacturer's promotional material.

The manufacturer's brochures show that it can be used for the development of colourways, final drawings and cost sheets. The students have used it for all these applications, but they also use it for their initial inspiration and a wide range of presentation material. Images scanned into the computer can be distorted and recoloured until they no longer resemble the original image. They can experiment with different silhouettes and textures. The final images can be printed on paper, acetate or a special paper which is used for iron-on transfers.

This system in particular has provided a user-friendly introduction to computers. The students are no longer wary of computers and are encouraged to investigate other systems. Philippa Eyland, a millinery student, has recently begun to use a standard three dimensional modelling package to develop the shapes for her hats. This innovative work would not have been possible without the introduction to computers provided by the systems in the fashion department.

The work done by these students shows what can be achieved when access to computers is provided. Their attitudes towards computers have changed through using them. They were initially apprehensive and did not know what to expect. Having used the systems they are now enthusiastic about them and demand to use them. They have developed their own methods of working on the systems and do not compromise their own individual ways of working. Several have expressed the hope that, when they leave college, they will be able to work for a company that provides computers for its designers.

Changing attitudes – whose responsibility?

There are many aspects of computers and their use which need to be improved in order to encourage a change in attitudes. The main problem is lack of access to the systems. When people can use systems they develop a more realistic attitude towards them, seeing them as everyday tools with their own limitations. Education is the obvious method of changing people's attitudes towards computers. For potential new users, especially those who have already left college, it is particularly difficult to obtain this.

An awareness of the subject, and the jargon that accompanies it, can be developed by reading articles, seeing demonstrations and attending seminars, but the only way to obtain a genuine understanding of the new technology is to use it. Without this practice the knowledge of the subject is meaningless. Training on specific systems is provided by the manufacturers and colleges. The manufacturers provide in-depth training for operators. The colleges usually provide an appreciation as part of their existing general courses. They may also provide shorter, more specific courses, similar to those already provided by the manufacturers, and sometimes aimed at people already in the industry.

Training in colleges

It is often forgotten that colleges have to face exactly the same problems with the introduction of computers as those faced by the industry. The problems of cost, personnel and attitudes are as relevant here as in the outside world; indeed they may be more of a problem. The cost of the systems is the same, but it cannot be justified by the normal savings to be made by computerisation. The personnel have to have all the same attributes as those required in industry, and they must also be enthusiastic teachers. The attitudes of everyone in the college are particularly important as these influence the attitudes of the students. All the tutors need to encourage their students to see the computer as a normal part of their work, not some specialist subject.

However, the colleges are in the business of training people and this involves extra, specific problems of its own. The intensive nature of training on computers causes particular problems when trying to teach large classes with already crowded timetables. Where installations in industry may be able to cope with a single-screen system, the colleges require many more work stations in order to accommodate the much larger number of users. These users have particular difficulties because they are learning the traditional skills at the same time as learning the computer. For this reason tuition on the systems is often slotted into the timetable as a separate course, distinct from other lessons, reinforcing the idea that computer skills are separate and not a normal skill for everyone. Hopefully this situation will change.

Students familiar with computers from school age will be able to concentrate on learning the more traditional techniques, and will use a computer as part of this.

If people already in the industry demand that colleges provide training for them in the application of computers, they will require separate courses from the existing students. Their knowledge of the traditional techniques gives them an advantage. The colleges will have to provide a range of courses suitable to the needs of all these different students. However, since they already experience difficulties with the available computer time, one wonders where they would be able to fit in these extra courses.

Industry's role

Education is not solely the responsibility of the colleges. Clothing and textile companies and computer manufacturers must take part in the activity of increasing people's awareness. They must be involved in college work to ensure that the courses are satisfying the demands of the industry. They could work with the colleges by setting specific projects as an initial support of computer-based work, thereby providing 'real' problems to solve. They also have further reponsibilities in changing people's attitudes.

If companies require their staff to be aware of computers they must be prepared to provide the time for training. It is too easy, in a busy production schedule, to make the excuse that there is not enough time to learn about computers. This leads to a situation where there is no incentive for experienced people to obtain this new information. The demand for computer training cannot be left until the purchase of a system and cannot stop with its purchase. Everyone in the company, as well as the operators, needs to be given the time to investigate its potential. In-house training should also be extended to the representatives of other companies who come into contact with the work from the computer.

Manufacturers' role

The computer manufacturers are competing to sell their own equipment. An increased awareness of the systems would be of particular benefit to them and they must play a major role in changing attitudes. They have always acknowledged the role that feedback from the industry has played in the development of their systems. They are eager to make changes to their programs when requested. However, unless the users of the computer are aware of the possibilities, they can only demand basic changes. The manufacturers must also listen to their potential, as well as existing, customers, especially with the new paintbox systems. Designers from different companies will have a range of uses for and opinions about these systems which must affect their development. Our leading designers must not be excluded from this.

All the systems could be improved by further software and hardware changes to make them more accessible to the new user. Computer manufacturers must develop the systems in such a way that people are encouraged to learn about them without being intimidated and finding them too difficult to approach. Improvements they make simplify training, encourage successful use and change people's attitudes.

Everyone involved with the clothing and textile industries has a responsibility in changing the attitudes towards computers. Colleges, companies and the manufacturers must all work together to encourage an awareness of the systems and provide easier access to them.

In conclusion

There are many exciting examples of the use of CAD systems in the clothing and textile industries. Outsiders appreciate that the normal tasks of stock control and wage processing are as likely to be performed by computer in these industries as in any other. But they still find it amazing that the whole manufacturing process, from the initial ideas through to the finished product, has involved the use of computers. It is tempting, particularly for those of us working with the systems, to assume that everyone within the industry has a full understanding of computer applications, but this is definitively not the case. Very few people have access to the systems, and negative attitudes still persist among the majority who have never used one.

In the rush to develop more powerful computer tools, we must not forget the opinions of these people. Just as computers become essential to the production process, everyone needs to become aware of the systems with their own ideas for future improvements. It is the responsibility of everyone involved with the clothing and textile industries to encourage a change in attitudes. There are current difficulties in obtaining knowledge about the systems because access to them is so limited, but this must not deter anyone. If there is a demand for computer training it will encourage the provision of suitable courses and the time to learn. I look forward to the day when everyone becomes a 'computer person' and that revolting term at last disappears from the design room.

Index